Old Salem

~ in ballad and song ~

Old Salem

~ in ballad and song ~

Part I

Old Salem at Sea ~ in ballad and song ~ Part II of the series

Researched and Compiled by

ROBERT E. STROM

Foreword by Jim McAllister

CABOT FARM PUBLISHER, SALEM, MASSACHUSETTS

Foreword

Salem, Massachusetts, is one of America's oldest and most historic small cities. Permanently settled in 1626, the coastal community later become famous for its architecture, maritime history, and connections to author Nathaniel Hawthorne - and infamous for its 1692 witch trials. Not surprisingly, "Historic Salem" today is a popular destination for tourists from all over the world.

Historians are especially fond of the city. Some are content to just walk the streets and visit the sites where Salem's history was made. Others research and write books about that history, most of them related to one of the afore-mentioned important Salem themes.

But many other deserving aspects of the city's past have been largely ignored by historians. Rare is the volume, for example, that pays tribute to Salem's lengthy and diverse musical heritage. A survey of my own shelves, crammed with nearly 200 full-length books and shorter publications, turns up a single pamphlet devoted to the topic. But that is finally about to change, thanks to the publication of Bob Strom's *Old Salem in Ballad and Song*.

When I met Bob twenty years ago, he was already a fixture on the Salem folk scene. When he wasn't working at his day job or gardening, Bob could usually be found playing guitar or stand-up bass at a local concert, contra dance, First Night celebration, Celtic or maritime festival or some other public event. He was usually joined on stage by his wife and fellow musician, Jennifer Strom, and other traditional "folkies" from the Greater Salem area. In addition to performing, the Stroms hosted or co-hosted folk "jam sessions" for fellow musicians. The couple also found time to produce a pair of albums, *'round the Bend* and *Heading Home*, of traditional songs from the British Isles and America.

Bob's longstanding immersion in, and passion for, the world of traditional folk songs and ballads paved the way for his new role as historian and author. Eight years ago, Strom began searching out "lost" or little-known works that had either been written or performed by Salemites or were based on people, places, or events from Salem's past. His internet research "travels" led him to the collections of the Library of Congress, Brown University, Middle Tennessee State University, Salem's Peabody Essex Museum and a host of other institutions. The author also drew on historical research previously undertaken by other musicians, most of them personal friends. John Allison, T. William Smith and the late Sarah Smith, Bob Franke, Larry Young, Jim Dalton and Maggie Smith-Dalton all shared gems they had uncovered in their own folk music treasure hunts. In some cases, their contributions were their own original Salem songs, like Bill Smith's *High Street* or Bob Franke's *Under the Willows*, or personal adaptions of older tunes or ballads.

The rich material Strom unearthed in his search laid the foundation for *Old Salem in Ballad and Song*. In his Introduction, the author briefly examines the role ballads and songs played in chronicling current events and saving them for posterity. The pages that follow are crammed with lyrics, verses, musical scores, illustrations and historical tidbits relating to works with Salem connections. Some names will be familiar to many readers. Strom notes that the famed 19th century bandleader Patrick Sarsfield Gilmore, who wrote the best-known version of *When Johnny Comes Marching Home*, led the Salem Brass Band from 1855 until 1858. The equally famous Hutchinson Family Singers performed at a New England Anti-Slavery Society convention held in Salem in 1844, and the group's temperance song *King Alcohol*, says the author, was inspired by the town's controversial Deacon Giles Distillery. And while Manuel Fenollosa is hardly a household name, the Salem composer's *Emancipation Hymn* (1863) was one of the most popular tunes of the Civil War era - at least in the northern states.

Also included in Strom's book are ballads related to the murder of Capt. Joseph White in 1831 (sung, ironically, to the tune of *Auld Lang Syne*), the pressing to death of Giles Corey during the 1692 witch trials and other tragic Salem events. The "Commerce" chapter features historical pieces like *The First Trip*, which was written for the opening celebration of the Salem-Lowell Railroad in 1850. The song was first sung at the event by the Salem Glee Club, one of the many 19th century musical societies and military bands highlighted by the author. Other songs reprinted in the book are downright fun and frivolous. The *Salem Willows for Mine* waltz (1919) captures the excitement and color of a popular park and amusement area on the Salem waterfront. *Chestnut Street*, written by Salem composer and four-term Salem mayor Henry Kemble Oliver, does the same for what has been called "the most beautiful street in America".

The above tidbits are offered as a sampling of the treasures to be found in the 209 pages of *Old Salem in Ballad and Song*. I enjoyed the book immensely: the combination of fascinating content, the author's style, and a plethora of illustrations make for easy and enjoyable reading. The book can be read piecemeal, and it doesn't require the reader to have to have a background in music or even local history. And the fact that few of the songs and ballads included in the ten themed chapters have much to do with Salem's witch trials, maritime history, architecture or Nathaniel Hawthorne means, obviously, that the reader is introduced to many new and different pieces of the Salem history "pie."

Old Salem in Ballad and Song will be a welcome addition to my Salem book collection, and a new and reliable (i.e. well footnoted) local history resource for which I am very grateful to Bob Strom.

There will be many times in the years to come that information gleaned from this book and his companion book *Old Salem at Sea in Ballad and Song*, will filter, with credit given of course, into my tours and lectures.

~ Jim McAllister

[Since 1983 Jim McAllister has been bringing Salem' history to life through tours, lectures, courses, and newspaper columns. He is the author of Salem From Naumkeag to Witch City and co-author of Salem Cornerstones of a Historic City. In 2015 he was designated Salem's Official Historian.]

Contents

Foreword   v

Introduction   xiii

I. SALEM

II. ON DYING, TRAGEDY

VI. COMMERCE

VII. DANCING

VIII. COURTSHIP

IX. CHILDREN SONGS

X. TEMPERANCE

Introduction

The 18th and 19th century ballad singer in Salem, Massachusetts was an important part of the community. Ballads of every theme from courtship to temperance were sung throughout the town, printed, and sold on the streets, and eventually spread around the country. The songs and ballads in this collection are rooted in Salem's history through oral and written tradition. Oral lore was passed along through songs and stories from one generation to another, while written traditions were well documented in broadside ballads, newspapers, posters, and manuscripts.

For the last several years, I have culled through numerous sources, mostly in the public domain, to collect material for this book. In selecting the material, I have limited the scope to ballads and broadsides, and to events in Salem not related to its maritime history. Part II of this two-book series, *Old Salem at Sea In Ballad and Song* will focus on Salem's maritime history.

Minstrel groups including the *Salem Cadet Minstrels*, the *Naumkeag Amateur Minstrels*, and the *Salem Amateur Minstrels*, who performed in the Salem area through the 18th and 19th centuries, were an integral part of the culture. And I have touched on some Minstrel song material, including *Ordway's Aeolians*, but have not gone into great depth.

I have also touched on Salem's long history of military and marching bands including Jean Missud's *Salem Assemblies Waltzes* but limited the amount of entries because this music is already well documented. Missud was known for writing the *March of the Salem Witches* and the *New Faneuil Hall March*. Later, George Rigby kept the marching band tradition alive from his predecessor Missud. That tradition continues today with bandleader Cynthia Napierkowski.

Ballads in this book can often be sung to airs or tunes familiar to the singer. Some of the lyrics have tunes associated with them while others do not and thus, give the singer freedom to create their own melodies to the words. On occasion, I have altered one or two words in a ballad for clarity and understanding.

The songs, ballads, and broadsides presented here describing specific events give a hint to Salem's past and its influence in helping to shape America both politically and socially.

Old Salem in Ballad and Song begins with Bob Franke's *Under the Willows*, which is a contemporary song describing the Salem Willows' seaside park. The book continues with a description of *The Pageant of Salem*, which portrays Salem as a *City of Peace* and then touches on events in Salem that affected social change, commerce, and war.

The Charlestown Land Shark is an example of a broadside ballad that brought about social change, while *Dreaming of Mother and Home* and the *Emancipation Hymn* were popular songs about the Civil War. The collection concludes with ballads that reflect the temperance movement that began in Salem and then spread throughout the country in the mid 19th Century. Each ballad holds a place in history that led to development and the growth of Salem, which today is a city notable for its rich culture as well for the tourism it attracts.

Harriet E. Peet who taught at the State Normal School (now Salem State University) in 1907 wrote an article titled *English Composition in the Elementary School: Studies in Ballad Literature*. She stated "the ballad tells its story in such a simple dramatic way that we have within it its charm of rhythm and rhyme and its echoes of far-off times." [1] The ballad, *Young Man of Salem: Execution of Stephen M. Clark* tells the story of a young sixteen-year-old boy who was hanged on Winter Island for the crime of arson, in 1821. [2]

Harriet Peet goes on to say:

> Long before printing had been invented and books and newspapers were common, strolling musicians went about from hamlet to hamlet in England and Scotland chanting old tales while accompanying themselves on harps or zithers. People gathered around these musicians on the village greens in the summer or in the chimney nook of a tavern or farmhouse on a wintery night. The listeners would often join in on the song's refrain or add a new verse. [1]

Imagine hearing William Warner or his agent selling Union Oil Polish to preserve boots inside local public houses or on the streets of Salem and Lynn while singing, *The New England Blacking Man* to the tune of *Yankee Doodle*.

> When Warner's agent went to Lynn,
> The polish'd men did hail him,
> They cheer'd him for the song he sang,
> And so they did in Salem.
>
> He sold a box and sung a verse,
> And then the dimes seemed handy,
> For people always like to hear
> Of Yankee Doodle Dandy. [3]

Redfern Mason wrote in his book, *The Song Lore of Ireland* that, "the rallying tune of the American Revolution *Yankee Doodle*, is an Irish air." [4] The air was originally called *All the Way to Galway*. Because copyright laws did not exist at the time, people wrote ballads and songs to familiar tunes. This was a common practice not only in Salem's bustling seaport town but also in most towns and cities throughout the new world and Europe.

When teaching her students about ballads, Harriet Peet wrote, "A ballad is a literary form almost perfectly adapted to children. But even a ballad, for all its simplicity, must have its method of presentation carefully thought out if it is to be used as a basis for study in a school room." [1]

We all remember the ditty *The Ants Go Marching One By One* for its humor and simplicity. Both the unforgettable tune and words meet Peet's criteria:

> The ants go marching one by one, Hurrah, Hurrah
> The ants go marching one by one, Hurrah, Hurrah
>
> The ants go marching one by one
> The little one stops to suck his thumb
> and they all go marching down to the ground
> To get out of the rain.

Patrick Gilmore, bandleader of the Salem Cadet Band, was inspired by the Battle of Gettysburg in 1863 and wrote the song *When Johnny Comes Marching Home*. There is ongoing debate about whether Gilmore originally heard the tune sung by hearing children sing it (*The Ants Go Marching One by One*) or by various minstrel groups, or whether it was a variant of one of Gilmore's Irish songs from his youth.[5] Either way, the song's popularity grew because of the sentiment for wanting to celebrate Johnny coming home from the Civil War no matter which side he fought on.

> The old church bell will peal with joy
> Hurrah! Hurrah!
> To welcome home our darling boy,
> Hurrah! Hurrah!
>
> The village lads and lassies say
> With roses they will strew the way,

And we'll all feel gay
When Johnny comes marching home.

As Salem moved into the mid 1800s so did copyright laws. The U.S. Supreme Court tried its first case relative to copyright law in 1834 some 44 years after the first copyright law was written. This act formalized the way music was written, presented and sold. Sheet music and songbooks were now copyrighted and published with royalties going directly to writers and publishers.

Manuel Fenollosa, a Spanish immigrant who immigrated to Salem, wrote the music for *Emancipation Hymn* in 1863. Oliver Ditson & Co. published the sheet music and Fenollosa received the royalties for his work. He continued to perform concerts throughout New England and in Salem after the Emancipation in 1864. The song, *Emancipation Hymn* reflects the times just after the Civil War:

Asking for a Land, for a Land united,
We forgot the slave.
Pray'd we for our Country, for our Country blighted--
For our falling brave.[6]

The ballads and songs in this book help tell the rich and fascinating story of Salem's past. Collecting material for this book has brought to light the ballad singer and the songs they sang. Each ballad tells a story about Salem in a way that can be remembered and retold. Some of these songs have been sung to familiar tunes while other songs have been copy written and sold throughout the land. The song tradition continues to live on today with contemporary songs written in the tradition of the past about Salem. I hope you get to know these ballads and sing these songs. Feel the rhythm of the tunes and share them with friends and family, but most of all enjoy the music.

~ Bob Strom

In Salem Town [7]

Quaint gabled house squat and frown
Along the streets in Salem Town,
And meeting elm-trees sway and nod
In memory of those who trod
The winding street in days gone by
When gay romance lured men to die.

What must they think the modern day
When things rush madly on their way
Along the streets in Salem Town
Where gabled houses squat and frown?

OLIVER JENKINS – 1922

Federal Street
In Salem, Mass
See gentle patience
Hope wipes the tear from sorrow's eye,

Salem

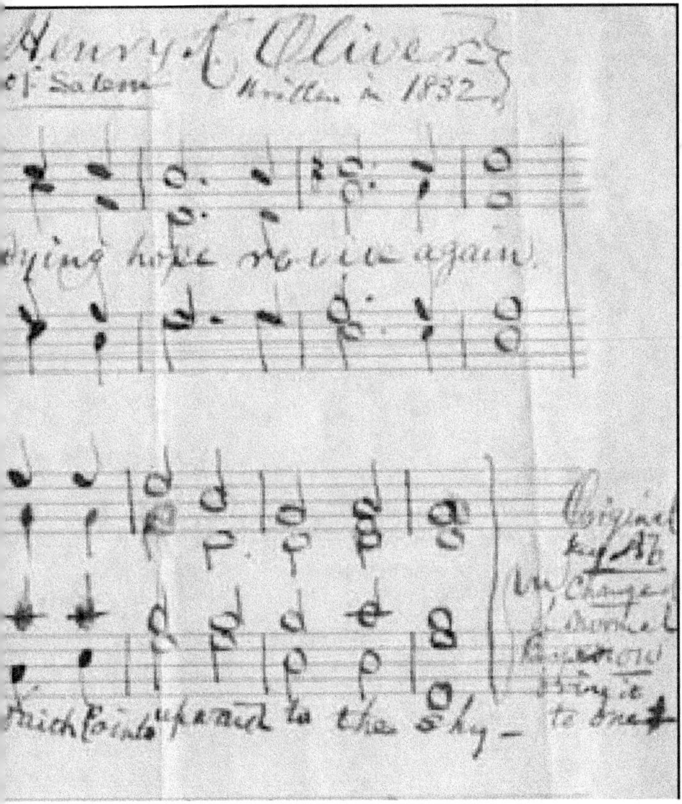

Henry K. Oliver

of Salem   Written in 1832

dying hope revive again,

which points upward to the sky —

Under The Willows

Under the Willows [1] was composed by Bob Franke and included on his *Brief Histories'* CD. It was written about Salem Willows, an historic seaside amusement park. Franke refers to the "old carousel," the "sweet Salem breeze," and the "Lemon Gibraltar" — an old-fashioned rock candy favorite. Eleanor Putman writes in her book *Old Salem*, "The Gibraltar is a white and delicate candy, flavored with lemon or peppermint, soft as cream at one stage of its existence, but capable of hardening into a consistency so stony and so unutterably flinty hearted that it is almost a libel upon the rock whose name it bears. The Gibraltar is the aristocrat of Salem confectionery." [2]

Franke currently lives in Peabody, Massachusetts and has been a popular folk singer in the states for over forty years.

Salem Willows Postcard,
courtesy of Sal Pangallo

Under The Willows

There's a spun-sugar smell in the penny arcade,
The old carousel is an endless parade;
Of horses and bunnies and camels and chicks,
Whose riders hang on to their peppermint sticks.

. Chorus: And it's under the willows come walk with me, love,
The sea at our feet and the sky up above.

The children at play know there's nothing to fear,
In the sweet Salem breezes, come walk with me, dear

See the bathers, so bold as their noses turn blue,
The young and the old build a castle or two;
Though the tide may bring tears when those castles depart,
There's a hope and a memory in each summer heart.

Chorus: And it's under the willows come walk with me, love,
The sea at our feet and the sky up above.
The children at play know there's nothing to fear,
In the sweet Salem breezes, come walk with me, dear.

Now, the rich merchant families look haughty and high,
But the big clipper packets have all passed us by;
And the captains of legend have all sailed away,
But they left us the sea and this fine summer day.

Chorus: And it's under the willows come walk with me, love,
The sea at our feet and the sky up above.
The children at play know there's nothing to fear,
In the sweet Salem breezes, come walk with me, dear.

Now, the storm clouds may roll on the wind far away,
But what's that to us on a day like today?
For the corn, it grows high; and the mill wheels still roll,
And the Lemon Gibraltar is good for the soul.

Chorus: And it's under the willows come walk with me, love,
The sea at our feet and the sky up above.
The children at play know there's nothing to fear,
In the sweet Salem breezes, come walk with me, dear

BOB FRANKE – 1992

Ode to Salem
City of Peace

Ode To Salem (City of Peace) was written by Alice Osborne Atwood and performed in The House of Seven the Gables Settlement Association's production of *The Pageant of Salem* in 1913. The Pageant was a weekend long event about the history of Salem beginning with the Naumkeag Indians, Roger Williams banishment by the government, the persecution of the Quakers, Salem's maritime commence, and the Witchcraft conflict. The production concluded with Salem's Nineteenth Century Days, and Nathaniel Hawthorne. [3]

In 1908, Caroline Emmerton purchased the Turner-Ingersoll mansion (now the House of the Seven Gables), had it restored, and opened the stately home to the public in 1910. [4] Emmerton used the proceeds from The House of the Seven Gables to fund the Settlement Association. The Settlement Association was considered a progressive organization that helped newly arriving immigrant families adapt to their new lives in the city [4]

Pageant of Salem Postcard,
courtesy of Sal Pangallo

Ode to Salem
City of Peace

Can sculptured stone or painted wood
Build up a city great and good?
How well the clear-eyed Greek replies;
"Where there are Men, the cities rise."

True men of faith, whose hearts are sure
That only things unseen endure;
So they toil on, by day and night,
Obedient to the Vision bright.

True men of love, who see the chain
Their brother wears, and feels his pain;
Who cannot rest, but run to share,
All that they have with Want and Care.

What though a city's numbers grow
When half are sunk in sin and woe?
What though her towers touch the sky,
Unless the thoughts of man be high?

O Salem! Let your children live
In peace the world can never give;
The peace of those who do God's will,
And see His kingdom coming still.

ALICE OSBORNE ATWOOD – 1913

The Pageant of Salem was one of the Settlement Associations' biggest fundraisers. During the pageant the song *Ode To Salem (City of Peace)* was sung to the tune of *Federal Street* written by Henry K. Oliver and was performed by the Salem Brass Band under the direction of Jean Missud.

Henry K. Oliver was born in Beverly, Massachusetts, on November 24, 1800 and died August 12, 1885. He served as the 21st Mayor of Salem from 1876 to 1880, was a member of the Massachusetts House of Representatives, an Adjutant General of Massachusetts, and also served as the 26th Treasurer of Massachusetts. Oliver lived at 142 Federal Street and was a master of the theory and history of music, and the author of several popular compositions. The tune *Federal Street* has become permanent in musical literature, and in sacred harp singing. [5]

Oliver taught school in Salem for almost 25 years (the Oliver School was named after him). He played organ at St. Peter's Church, and led the choir at the North Church in Salem. *Oliver's Collection of Church Music,* and *Dr. Tuckerman's the National Lyre* are examples of his work. Oliver was also a member of the Salem Glee Club. [6]

Henry K. Oliver, *Seventeenth Annual Report of the Bureau of Statistics of Labor (1886),* courtesy of the Salem Public Library

The Origin of the "Salem Shag"

The origins of the *Salem Shag* are unclear but according to Huntress & Dennis Aylward, in an article in the *Essex Institute Collection*, a New York philologist summering in Salem said, "he was unwilling to go home until he had discovered the origin of the *Salem Shag*." The Essex Institute could not find a better explanation to offer him than these verses. [7]

In martial panoply arrayed,
Welcomed of sire, beloved of maid,
See our brave youngsters file in view,
What time the century was new, —

The gilded youth of Salem town,
In leggins white, with muskets brown,
Coats blue, picked out in dainty red.
Casques fit to cap a Spartan's head,

High topped with nodding ostrich plume
White as the angry ocean's foam.
While each proud crest must flaunt in air
Its shaggy tuft of blood-red hair.

As though in gore some battle-steed
His streaming mane had drenched indeed.
Thus bravely 'dight for war or love,
To muster marched, — in ball-room strove, —

The youth of Salem's halcyon time.
Proud striplings of our golden prime,
So shaggy, all who saw them swore,
"These should be shags" — and shags they were!

TRADITIONAL – 1894

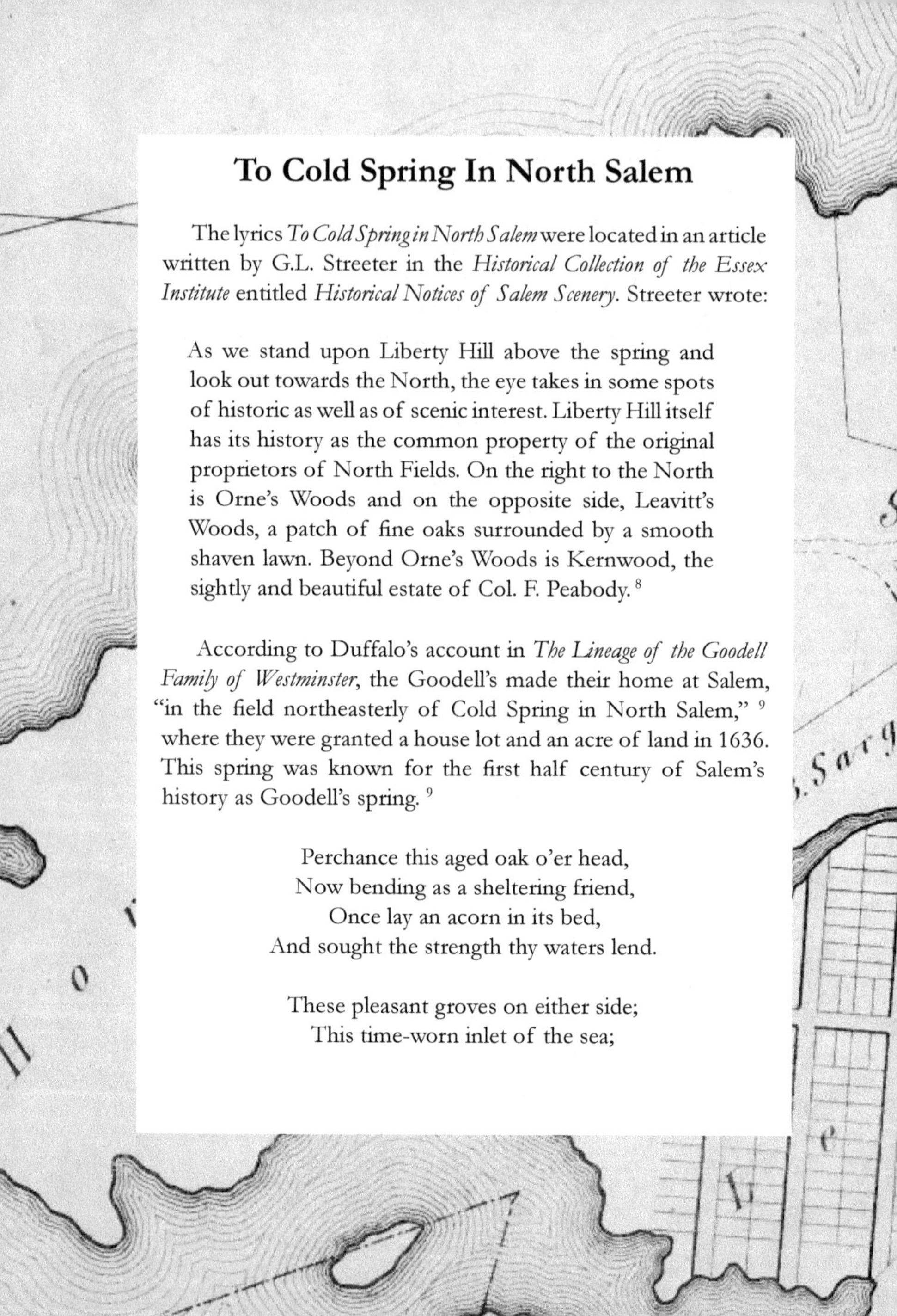

To Cold Spring In North Salem

The lyrics *To Cold Spring in North Salem* were located in an article written by G.L. Streeter in the *Historical Collection of the Essex Institute* entitled *Historical Notices of Salem Scenery*. Streeter wrote:

As we stand upon Liberty Hill above the spring and look out towards the North, the eye takes in some spots of historic as well as of scenic interest. Liberty Hill itself has its history as the common property of the original proprietors of North Fields. On the right to the North is Orne's Woods and on the opposite side, Leavitt's Woods, a patch of fine oaks surrounded by a smooth shaven lawn. Beyond Orne's Woods is Kernwood, the sightly and beautiful estate of Col. F. Peabody. [8]

According to Duffalo's account in *The Lineage of the Goodell Family of Westminster*, the Goodell's made their home at Salem, "in the field northeasterly of Cold Spring in North Salem," [9] where they were granted a house lot and an acre of land in 1636. This spring was known for the first half century of Salem's history as Goodell's spring. [9]

Perchance this aged oak o'er head,
Now bending as a sheltering friend,
Once lay an acorn in its bed,
And sought the strength thy waters lend.

These pleasant groves on either side;
This time-worn inlet of the sea;

Yon swelling bills that stay the tide;
All share their life and years with thee.

Here once the Indian loved to quaff
Thy cooling bowl, in summer's day;
To see thy wavelets dance and laugh;
And watch thy sands in mimic play.

Yet now, as then.—so long ago—
Thy tiny fountains flood the brim;
Thy singing waters seaward go,—
A rill of praise, a constant hymn.

Thou art a joy, a gift divine.
Thy cup o'er flows for every lip;
The timid bird, the thirsty kind,
The weary traveler, stoop to sip.

Gush ever forth, thou ancient Spring!
Refresh, delight, inspire the heart.
Thou art, indeed, a lovely thing,
But faithful to thy humble part.

TRADITIONAL – 1800s

Jones Very who was born and raised in Salem also wrote a poem about the springs in North Salem entitled *To Cold Spring in North Salem.* [10] The first verse begins:

0, sweet, refreshing, bubbling fount!
The tribute of this ancient hill.
No human heart can hope to count
How long has flowed thy generous hill?

Smoking - on 76 Chestnut Street

Smoking - on 76 Chestnut Street [11] was found in the log journal of the *Ship Ringleader* based in Boston. Its writer Edwin Humphreys from Salem wrote this song about smoking and refers to 76 Chestnut Street in Salem in the lyrics.

Chestnut Street Postcard, courtesy of Sal Pangallo

The homes on Chestnut Street were built by wealthy sea captains during the 1800s. To this day Chestnut Street is considered "The most beautiful street in America." It is the address of Hamilton Hall, which has been an assembly hall for cultural and social events for over 200 years, and it is also the address of the historic Phillips House located on 34 Chestnut Street. According to The Registry of Deeds, [12] 76 Chestnut Street in Salem does not exist because numbered houses only go up to 48. The house 76 Chestnut Street in Humphrey's song may actually be located in Boston, since a house was built on Boston's 76 Chestnut Street during that time. We'll let the mystery be.

Smoking, many people say,
Is good to drive the blues away.
It makes men social, drowns their cares,
To puff their troubles in the air
But to be brief and stop all joking,
There's nothing (taste) like Goodwin's smoking.

Just so with chewing – all, of every rank,
Use Goodwin's celebrates Yellow Bank.
Tis lively, bright and full of juice,
The best tobacco now in use.

Others with habits firmly fixed,
Prefer the Sarsaparilla mixed.
He say 'tis of the finest grade,
And knocks all others in the shade.

To all the various brands you'll find,
Of every shade and every kind.
But none superior on the list,
To convert's celebrated twist.

You know all men of every creed,
Who use this most delicious weed?
The place to find it all complete,
Is 76 on Chestnut Street.
Salem, Mass.

EDWIN HUMPHREYS – 1858

Observations of Their Travel

Roger Williams was born in London circa 1603 and died in March of 1683. Williams was a minister who founded the first Baptist Church (Meeting House) in America in 1638. He worked closely with Native Americans in New England and wrote the first dictionary of Native American languages. Williams was banished from Salem because of his separatist teachings. As voiced in the *Christian Pioneer Intended To Uphold The Great Doctrines of the Reformation*, a book of unknown authorship, "God can comfort, feed and safely guide even through a desolate howling wilderness." [13] After his exile from Salem in mid-winter, ill and on his way to form the colony of Rhode Island and Providence Plantations, pilgrim poet Roger Williams [13] wrote these verses in 1643:

God makes a path, provides a guide,
And feeds in wilderness;
His glorious name while earth remains,
Oh that I may confess.

Lost many a time I've had no guide,
No house but hollow tree;
In stormy winter night no fire,
No food no company.

In him I have found a house, a bed,
A table company;
No cup so bitter but's made sweet,
When God shall sweetening be. [14]

ROGER WILLIAMS – 1643

In 1829, Job Dufree (1790 – 1847) of Tiverton, Rhode Island wrote *Roger Williams in Banishment: The Fire-Side of Salem*. Durfee, a Rhode Island politician, decided not to run for a re-election and retired to private life and "mingled with agricultural labors and the more delightful pursuits of literature." [15] It was during his retirement that he wrote the epic poem *Roger Williams in Banishment*. The poem is an account of the journey of Mr. Williams through the wilderness, his subsequent first settlement in Seekonk, Massachusetts, and his later settlement in Providence. [16] Verses 1 and 3 are included here.

Whatcheer or Roger Williams in Banishment
The Fire-Side of Salem

I sing of trials stern and sufferings great,
Which Father Williams in his exile bore,
That he the conscience bound might liberate,
And her religious rights the soul restore;
How after flying persecution's hate,
And roving long by Narragansett's shore,
In lone Moshassuck's vale at last he sate,
And gave soul liberty her Guardian State.

Midwinter reigned and Salem's town,
Where late were cleft the skirts away,
Showed its low roofs and from thatching brown,
The sheeted ice sent back the last ray;
The schoolboys left the slippery crown,
So keen the blast came o'er the bay.
And the fun in vapors thick down,
And the glassed forest cast a sombre frown.

JOB DURFEE – 1829

Salem Hornpipe

On The Road To Salem Quickstep

Patrick S. Gilmore wrote the *Salem Hornpipe* [17] in 1853. Jim Dalton a Salem resident, and Professor of Core Studies at Boston Conservatory at Berklee, unearthed an early written version of the tune at the Boston Public Library. He discovered that the *Salem Hornpipe* was part of a longer piece called *On The Road To Salem Quickstep*. Dalton stated in an article written in the *Salem Gazette*, "the names of the officers were listed in order of rank, right on the music as if Gilmore was dedicating a few beats of the music to each." [18] Dalton continued looking for the connection and he noticed, "on the fourth page of the music, it was labeled *Road to Salem*, the same tune as the *Salem Hornpipe*." [18]

Salem Hornpipe, courtesy of Jim and Maggi Dalton's private collection

Gilmore soon became leader of the Salem Brass Band between the years 1855 and 1858 when it developed into one of the finest bands in the country. The *Salem Hornpipe* can also be found in William Bradbury *Ryan's Mammoth Collection: 1050 Reels and Jigs* originally published by Elias Howe in Boston in 1883.

Jim and his wife, Maggi Smith-Dalton performs 19th and 20th century American music.

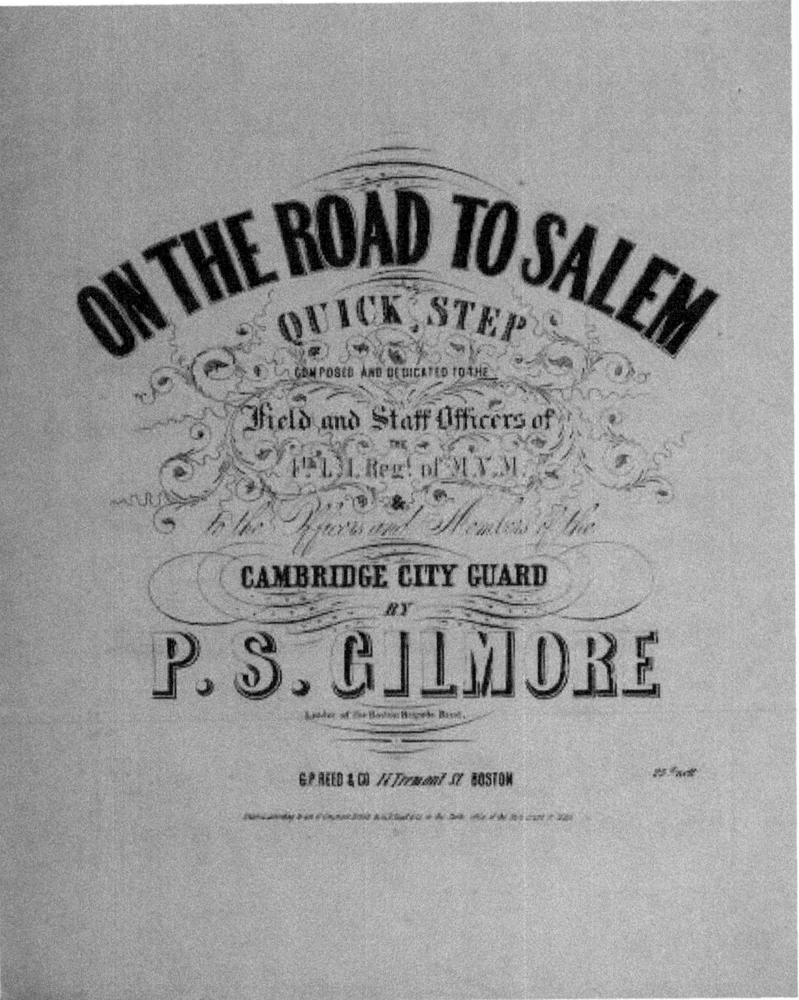

On the Road to Salem, courtesy of the Boston Public Library

Salem Artillery

The *Salem Artillery* [19] was a popular dance and military tune played in Salem around 1800. The tune was researched and transcribed by T. William Smith, a Salem resident and folk musician, circa 1980. It was discovered at the Essex Institute and played regularly by the Salem Country Orchestra at contra dances in Salem between the years 1985 and 2010.

TRADITIONAL – 1800

Be Salem Home

Be Salem Home was culled from the *Essex Register* [20] dated
March 17, 1826. By 1826, the wars with England are over and the
embargo is lifted. Salem, economically is flourishing with shipping,
trade, manufacturing, and the arts. The sentiment of Salem and the
country is reflected in the last line of the song, 'Tis wise, and good,
to live and die in Peace.

Be Salem home. 'Tis sweet to live in Peace
Where commerce flourishes, and trade increase;
Where manufacture germs in fertile fields,
Which, rightly cultured, rich abundance yields.

Where intellect exuberantly springs,
Amidst examples of life's useful things;
Where Pageantry is not the Idol serv'd;
But Industry to worth intrinsic nerv'd.

Where few amusements, lavish, or of chance
Impede the Arts and Sciences advance;
Where blest Religion reigns, with conscience free
For all to differ, who cannot agree,

To fit the soul
    for duty and release,
'Tis wise, and good,
    to live and die in Peace.

ALFRED – 1826

Essex Register, March 17, 1826,
courtesy of Christine Elizabeth
Mistretta's private collection.

THERE'S CRAPE ON THE

DEXTER SMITH.

"It is appointed unto men once to die."—H

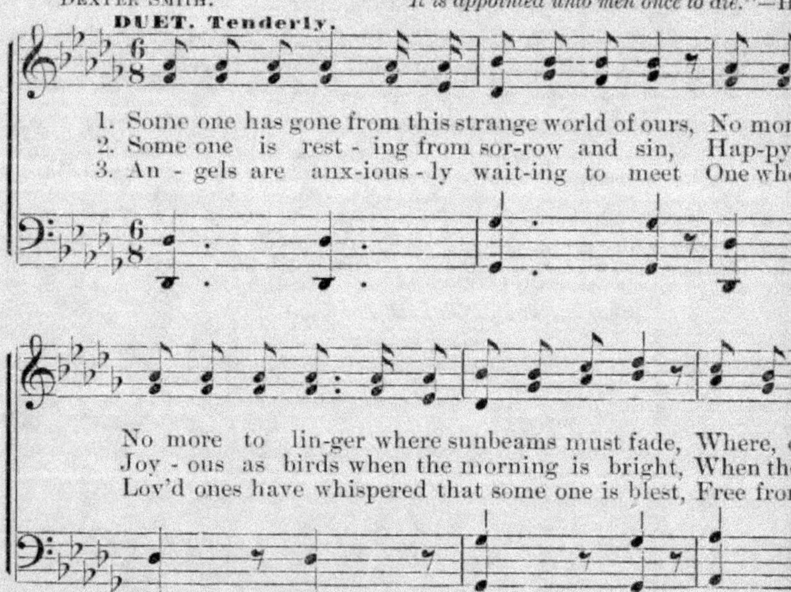

~ 2 ~

On Dying and Tragedy

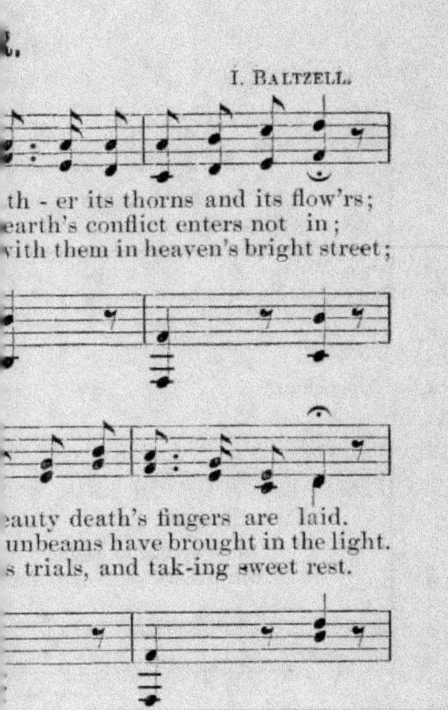

Written on reading an account of the execution of

Stephen M. Clark

The broadside, *Written on reading an account of the execution of Stephen M. Clark* was found in the Harris Broadside Collection at the John Hay Library at Brown University.[1] The jury found Clark guilty and recommended commutation of his sentence, but the state hanged Stephen Merrill Clark. He was executed on Winter Island in Salem on Thursday the tenth day of May 1821 at the early age of 16 years and 9 months, for the crime of arson.[2]

Clark's case fueled the movement in Massachusetts to reduce the number of capital crimes, if not abolish the death penalty altogether. By 1852, only murder remained on the books as a capital offense. In 1984, the Supreme Judicial Court ruled the death penalty unconstitutional.[3]

> OH! Massachusetts! Name to me most dear,
> And Salem too, thou art my native spot,
> For thee I have to drop pitying tear,
> For on thy name there's a disgraceful blot.
>
> Oh! Could'st thou not thy legal arm outstretch,
> Show mercy to the Youth who now is gone,
> Snatch from the grave the poor deluded wretch,
> And mitigate the grief of those who mourn?
>
> Could not this Youth-could not the hoary hairs
> Of his afflicted broken-hearted sire,
> Could not a People's cries, a People's prayers,
> A human breast with pity's glow inspire?

Me thinks I see the afflicted Father stand,
His quivering lips, his stammering tongue employ,
To implore the ruler of a pious land,
To spare this guilty but repenting boy.

But all his supplications were in vain,
Mercy was due, but mercy was denied,
Nothing an Earthly pardon could obtain,
Die, says the law-the young offender dies.

Here ends the scene-his spirit now is flown,
Unto that God by whom, all crimes are tried,
And there I trust that mercy will be shown,
Which unrelenting man on earth denied.

WRITTEN BY A YOUNG MAN OF SALEM – 1831

LINES

Written on reading an account of the execution of

STEPHEN M. CLARK.

BY A YOUNG MAN OF SALEM.

OH ! MASSACHUSETTS ! name to me most dear,
 And Salem too, thou art my native spot,
For thee I have to drop a pitying tear,
 For on thy name there's a disgraceful blot.

Oh ! could'st thou not thy legal arm outstretch,
 Show mercy to the Youth who now is gone,
Snatch from the grave the poor deluded wretch,
 And mitigate the grief of those who mourn ?

Could not this Youth—could not the hoary hairs
 Of his afflicted broken-hearted sire,
Could not a People's cries, a People's prayers,
 A human breast with pity's glow inspire ?

Methinks I see the afflicted Father stand,
 His quivering lips, his stammering tongue employ,
To implore the ruler of a pious land,
 To spare his guilty but repenting boy.

But all his supplications were in vain,
 Mercy was due, but mercy was denied,
Nothing an Earthly pardon could obtain,
 Die, says the law—the young offender dies,

Here ends the scene—his spirit now is flown,

George A. Brown

The ballad of *George A. Brown* was composed and sung to the tune of *Pleyel's Hymn* at his grave. George Brown drowned in Salem on February 18, 1857. [4] The text was found in the Broadside Collection, at the Center for Popular Music, at Middle Tennessee State University.

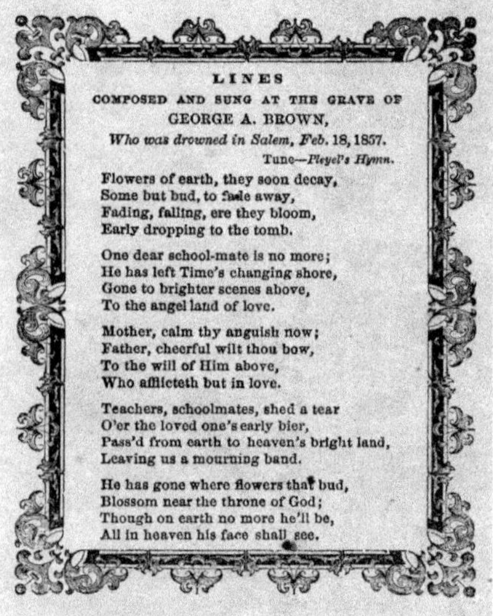

George A. Brown, courtesy of the Kenneth S. Goldstein Collection of American Song Broadsides Center for Popular Music, Middle Tennessee State University

Flowers of earth, they soon decay,
Some but bud, to fade away.
Fading, falling, ere they bloom,
Early dropping to the tomb.

One dear school-mate is no more;
He has left Time's changing shore,
Gone to brighter scenes above,
To the angel land of love.

Mother, calm thy anguish now;
Father, cheerful wilt thou bow,
To the will of Him above,
Who affecteth but in love.

Teacher, schoolmates, shed a tear,
O'ver the loved one's early bier,
Pass'd from earth to heaven's bright land,
Leaving us a mourning band.

He has gone where flowers that bud,
Blossom near the throne of God,
Though on earth no more he'll be,
All in heaven his face shall see.

TRADITIONAL – 1857

A Funeral Elegy

A Funeral Elegy is a ballad about seven women and three men who tragically drowned in Salem in June of 1773 while out on a "party of pleasure" to Baker's Island. [5] According to Raymond H. Bates Jr. in his book: *Shipwrecks North of Boston, Volume I, Salem Bay*, the group sailed aboard the Salem Custom House Boat called "the King's Boat," a large two-mastered vessel. During the afternoon the weather began to turn dark—foreboding clouds and strong gusts of wind developed. [6] "As the King's Boat cruised by Eagle Island, an intense gust of wind hit the sail hard." [6] The boat began sank and only two persons were saved.

Baker's Island Postcard, courtesy of Sal Pangallo

Awake, my Muse, and tune the Song
To harp a doleful sound,
Enough to melt the mournful Throng,
Which echoes oe'r the Ground.

What Heart but feels the heavy Stroke
Sent by GOD's awful Hand,
When ten poor Souls were lately cast
Ashore upon the Sand.

Think, O poor Salem, think upon,
And hear this dreadful Thing,
Ne'r let it pass without regret;
But fear your heav'nly King.

Yes, ten poor Souls, I've heard them say
Went lately to the Bottom: Salem,
O let it not be said
Their Names were e'er forgotten.

May we not say fifteen poor Souls
Were plunged in the Sea,
As Five th' unhappy Women were
Advanc'd in Pregnancy.

A shocking Sight must it not seem,
And dismal for to see
The loving Husband and the Wife
Who once did well agree?

Now they embrace each other's Arms,
And take a watery Grave;
All Nature sure it must alarm
To see that men can't save.

O who could bear to hear the Shrieks
And Cries none could prevent
Among these wretched dismal Souls,
It makes my heart relent.

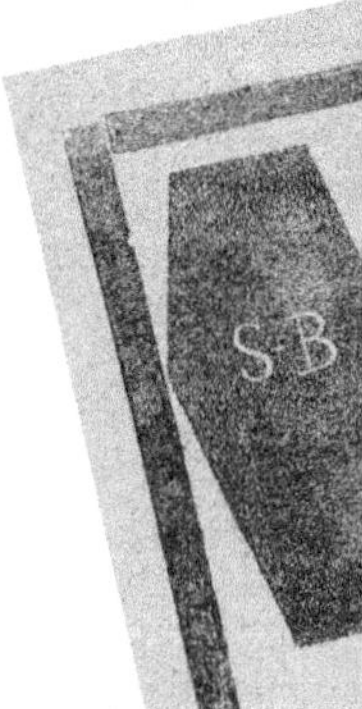

The tender Hand of Help was near,
No Help it could afford,
Though Friends were nigh, behold and cry
They could not get aboard.

May grateful Thanks be ever paid
To Marblehead's kind Town;
Whose Hearts relent, their Strength they
And sav'd two Souls not drown'd.

When Gentle, Simple, all agree
To lend an aiding Hand,
With Heart and Voice they now rejoice
To form a helping Band.

Their pitying Hand was kindly shewn,
May it remember'd be.
When Friends, Relatives, Neighbours were
So late drown'd in the Sea.

The dismal Boat and Relicts they
With much adieu did save,
To Salem Wharf they landed them,
For which kind Thanks they have.

Alas, who then but grieves and mourns,
With Many a sigh and Tear,
Beholding of their dismal Urns,
Their Corpse is drawing near.

Hark, Hark! We hear the passing Bell,
Along as they do go;
Traveller, stop and shed a Tear;
This is a Scene of Woe.

TRADITIONAL – 1773

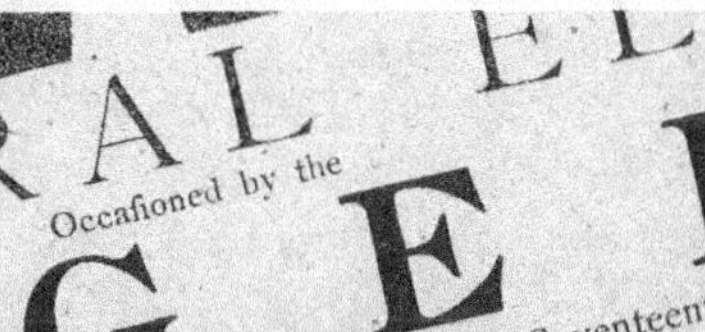

Murder of Joseph White

The *Murder of Joseph White* was found in the Harris Broadside Collection at Brown University and is sung to the tune of *Auld Lang Syne*. The murder of Joseph White was the subject of the book titled *Death of an Empire, The Rise and Murderous Fall of Salem, America's Richest City* by Robert Booth. [7]

O WHAT a horrid tale of sound,
In this our land to tell,
That Joseph White, of Salem town,
By ruffian hands he fell!
Perhaps for money or for gain,
This wicked deed was done;
But it for either, great the pain,
This monster must be in.

O thou infernal of the damned,
To murder in the night,
With cruel arm and blood-stained hand,
Which pierced the side of White;
Thou hardened-hearted monster devil,
To thrust the dirk of death,
You will be placed upon the level,
For time will stop your breath!

There you will lie, 'the trump will sound,'
And God will call you forth;
You will be judged, and then be bound,
In weighty chains of wrath,
And doomed to that infernal place,
Where devils have their train,

You must be paid by devil's grace,
With torture, anguish, pain.

What led you to this awful deed,
No man on earth can tell;
But may we know, God give it speed,
That you may flee from hell.
O that the mighty Arm above,
Would bring to light the wretch,
And on his soul might rest the Dove
That gave this sinner breath.

Who would have thought that such a deed,
In this, our Christian land,
Would e'er have taken place, indeed!
It has, O cruel hand!
To slay an aged gentleman,
No person he could harm,
In murder shocking, in extreme,
While he lay sleeping calm.

Calmly he laid in sweet repose,
That ruffian forced the room,
And with his dirk he did dispose,
Of him, who'd done no harm.
Greta God, how can these things be so!
When man is left alone,
Poor feeble wretch, he does not know,
How wicked he has done.

The restraining grace of Heaven,
Will keep us all from wrong,

But O, that cursed hellish leaves,
It leavens, to be strong,
Like devils, for destruction bold,
And wealth and blood their aim,
And to all good their hearts are cold,
Care not for heavenly claims.

O! Did you think you were concealed?
No; no, there's one could see,
And sure the crime will be revealed,
This side of eternity,
And banish him, that cursed wretch,
Into that dark abode,
Where devils fight; think not of wealth,
And he will join their code.

For he has been a Brutus bold,
Without the fear of God,
To heavenly precepts he is cold,
He thirsts for wealth and blood.
He has effected a design,
To him will prove a curse;
He may be dropped from the platform,
Or doomed to something worse.

Great Pope once said that all was 'right,'
So said a sturdy thief;
But when he found a rope, he might
Have altered his belief;
And so would say that artful wretch,
Who murdered Joseph White-
The hangman he may stop his breath,
And prove that Pope was 'right.'

TRADITIONAL – 1830

Murder of Joseph White.

The following lines were written on the death of MR. JOSEPH WHITE, of Salem, who was found murdered in his bed, on the morning of the 7th of April, 1830, aged 82 years.

" Shall auld acquaintance be forgot, and never brought to mind ?
Shall ' horrid murder' be forgot, in the days of Auld Lang Syne ;
No : let this tale be treasur'd up, that one and all may know,
That they taste not the bitter cup, of sin, and death, and woe.

TUNE—' *Auld Lang Syne.*'

O WHAT a horrid tale to sound,
  In this our land to tell,
That JOSEPH WHITE, of Salem Town,
By ruffian hands he fell !
Perhaps for money, or for gain,
This wicked deed was done,
But if for either, great the pain
This monster must be in.

O thou infernal of the damn'd,
To murder in the night,
With cruel arm, and blood-stain'd hand,
Which pierc'd the side of *White.*
Thou harden'd hearted, monster devil,
To thrust the *dirk* of death,
You will be plac'd upon the level,
For time will stop your breath !

There you will lie, the ' *tramp will sound,*'
And God will call you forth ;
You will be judg'd, and then be bound
In weighty chains of wrath ;
And doom'd to that infernal place
Where devils have their train,
You will be paid, by devils' *grace,*
With torture, anguish, pain.

What led you to this awful deed,
No man on earth can tell ;
But may we know, God give it speed,
That you may flee from *Hell.*
O! that the Mighty arm above,
Would bring to light the wretch,
And on his soul might rest the Dove,
That gave this sinner breath.

Who would have thought that such a deed,
In this, our Christian land,
Would ever taken place, indeed ;
It has, O! cruel hand.
To slay an aged gentleman,
No person he could harm,
Is murder shocking, in extreme.
While lay sleeping calm

Calmly he laid in sweet repose,
The ruffian forc'd the room,
And with his dirk, he did dispose
Of him, who'd done no harm.
Great God, how can these things be so ?
When man is left alone,
Poor feeble wretch, he does not know
How wicked he has done.

The restraining grace of Heaven,
Will keep us all from wrong,
But O, that cursed, hellish leaven,
It *leavers,* to be strong.
Like devils, for destruction bold,
And wealth and blood their aim,
And to all good their hearts are cold.
Care not for heavenly claim.

Did you think you were conceal'd ?
No ; no, there's ONE could see,
And sure the crime will be reveal'd,
This side of eternity.
And banish him, that cursed wretch,
Into that dark abode,
Where *Devils* fight ; think not of wealth,
And he will join their code.

For he has been a Brutus bold,
Without the fear of God,
To heavenly precepts he is cold,
He thirsts for wealth and blood.
He has effected a design
To him will prove a curse :
He may be dropt from the *platform,*
Or doom'd to something worse.

Great Pope once said, that all was ' right,'
So said a sturdy thief ;
But when he found a rope, he might
Have ' alter'd his belief,'
And so would say that artful wretch,
Who murder'd Joseph White—
The hangman he may stop his breath,
And prove that Pope was ' right.'

Sold Wholesale and Retail, corner of Merchants' Row & Market Square, Boston.

Ballad of Giles Corey

The *Ballad of Giles Corey* [8] is a shortened version of *Giles Corey & Goodwyfe Corey, A Ballad of 1692.* [9] In 1962, John Allison recorded the shortened version called the *Ballad of Giles Corey* on his LP *Witches and War-Whoops: Early New England Ballads.* According to an article in the *Essex Institute Bulletin* called *The Witchcraft Delusion in New England,* the ballad was first published in the April 13, 1850 issue of the *Salem Observer* and was written by Fitch Poole, Esquire of Peabody.

The Ballad of Giles Corey

Giles Corey was a Wizard strong,
A stubborn wretch was he;
And fit was he to hang on high,
Upon the Locust-Tree.

So when before the magistrates,
For trial he did come;
He would no confession make,
But was completely dumb.

"Giles Corey," said the Magistrate,
What hast thou here to plead;
To those who now accuse thy soul,
Of crime and horrid deed?"

Giles Corey he said not a word,
No single word spoke he.
Giles Corey," said the Magistrate,
"We'll press it out of thee."

They got them then a heavy beam.
They laid it on his breast;
They loaded it with heavy stones,
And hard upon him pressed.

"More weight!" Now said this wretched man;
"More weight!" Again he cried;
And he did no confession make,
But wickedly he dyed.

FITCH POOLE – 1850

The long version of the ballad of *Giles Corey & Goodwyfe Corey,
A Ballad of 1692* begins:

Come all New England Men
And hearken unto me
And I will tell what did befalle
Upon ye Gallows Tree.

In Salem Village was the place
As I did heare them saye
And Goodwyfe Corey was her name
Upon that paynfull daye.

This Goody Corey was a Witch
The People did believe
Afflicting of the Godly Ones
Did make them fadlie Greave. [9]

Ring The Bell Softly,
There's Crape on the Door

Dexter Smith wrote the ballad *Ring The Bell Softly, There's Crape on the Door* in 1867. Smith was born in Salem, on November 14, 1837. Smith became a postman in Boston after graduating from a college in Boston. While delivering mail to a particular house,

Dexter Smith from the *Phrenological Journal and Life Illustrated*

he noticed black crape paper draped around the doorknob, which was a sign of mourning. He approached the home and the sign said, "not to disturb the sorrowing occupants" and delivered the mail as quietly as possible. [10] Smith soon after wrote the song *Ring The Bell Softly; There's Crape on the Door.*

Some one has gone from this strange world of ours
No more to gather its thorns with its flowers
No more to linger where sunbeams must fade
Where, on all beauty, Death's fingers are laid

Chorus: Weary with mingling Life's bitter and sweet
    Weary with parting and never to meet
    Some one has gone to the bright golden shore
    Ring the bell softly, there's crepe on the door.
    Ring the bell softly, there's crepe on the door.

Someone is resting from sorrow and sin
Happy where earth's conflicts enter not in
Joyous as birds, when the morning is bright
When the sweet sunbeams have brought us their light

Chorus: Weary with sowing and never to reap
         Weary with labour and welcoming sleep
         Someone's departed to Heaven's glad shore
         Ring the bell softly, there's crepe on the door.
         Ring the bell softly, there's crepe on the door.

Angels are anxiously longing to meet
One who walks with them in Heaven's bright street
Loved ones have whispered that someone is blest
Free from earth's trials, and taking sweet rest

Chorus: Yes, There's one more in angelic bliss
         One less to cherish, and one less to kiss
         One more departed to Heaven's bright shore
         Ring the bell softly, there's crepe on the door.
         Ring the bell softly, there's crepe on the door.

DEXTER SMITH – 1867

Ring The Bell Softly became very popular and was published in nearly every newspaper and magazine in America and England. "Had Dexter Smith never written any other poem *Ring The Bell Softly* would have established his reputation as a true poet and secured to him a high niche in temple of Fame" [11] Smith continued to write songs that "served to cheer the patriot heart and to encourage those who took up arms to defend the banner of our country." [12] He wrote songs titled: *Follow the Drum, Our Boys in Camp,* and *Hurrah for the Old Flag* that are all in the patriotic vein. Smith went on to publish a book of poetry, called *Dexter Smith's Poems* [13] in 1868. Dexter died on November 28, 1909.

HARMONY GROVE.

~ 3 ~

Imprisoned

The Escape of Old John Webb

or Billy Broke Locks

John Roberts, a folk singer from the British Isles, now living in New York, sang The *Escape Of Old John Webb* at Larry Young's session at O'Neil's Irish Pub in Salem, Massachusetts in 2003. Since John was playing in Salem, he wanted to sing a Salem song. Several years later, while speaking with John about the song, he said he learned, his version from the *Kingston Trio* and added lyrics from Phillips Barry's *British Ballads from Maine*.[2]

Singer-songwriter and lyricist for the *Kingston Trio*, Tom Drake, posted a thread to the *Kingston Trio* forum *On Top Of Old Folkie* on February 5, 2000 explaining how he adapted the song *The Escape of Old John Webb* in order to record it on an upcoming *Kingston Trio* album. Tom said, "The post was in response to multiple posts by others speculating on the origins/authorship of *The Escape of Old John Webb*."[1] Tom spent a few days in the library researching songs for his next album, and the song *John Webb* made it to the top of the pile.

Tom went on to write the linking verses to tell a linear story. Then the recording studio called Tom and said that there was no copyright on the song so they were putting him down as the writer.[1] Tom went on to say, "The revision of public domain material is an established and vital part of the folk process. You take what you hear and you bring it up to date."[1]

Versions of the song can be found in Phillips Barry's *British Ballads from Maine*,[2] *The Burl Ives' Songbook*,[3] and in Alan Lomax's *The Folk Songs of North America*.[4] Both Burl Ives and Alan Lomax made reference to a 1730s article about the event and how John Webb was jailed in Salem around 1730 for the crime of counterfeiting. His imprisonment was unpopular and a mob set him free. Phillips says, "At the time, exchange in the colonies was based upon Spanish coinage."[2]

Last Monday, towards evening a Man, whose Name is since found to be John Webb, of Salem came to the shop of Mr. Lass.... Casno Sadler, upon the Town Dock, and cheapened a saddle which being agreed for, he offer'd a Five Pound Bill from the Colony of Rhode Island for pay, but the bill being scripted by Mr. Casno, and censured as a Counterfeit by several Persons who happened to be present, the Man left the Bill, mounted his horse, and rode away with such Expedition that he had Like to have run over several persons in the street, as he headed out of town. [6]

The next day he was pursed by an Officer who had the good fortune to take him at Providence, and about twelve o'clock Wednesday night he was brought to Town, in custody of the officer and another man to assist him. The office should have committed him to prison, but he begg'd so hard that he be kept at the Officer's house that at last his request was granted, but about five o'clock in the morning he threw up the sash, jump'd out the window and so made his escape. [6]

The officer not a little unsettled to be shunned But with to Chris Lenfy went in quest of him again the next day, and was so lucky, as to find him in his Mother's garden at Salem. He had provide himself with arms, apprehended to stand on his defense but after some time he was taken and committed to Goal there... [6]

Article referring to *John Webb, Boston Evening Post*, Monday, October 16, 1738, courtesy of the Boston Public Library.

When England replaced the old tenor with new tenor, "John Webb then mint-master of Salem, apparently stuck to the old tenor and for this offense was sent to prison. His friends broke into the jail and rescued Webb" [2]

In the ballad book *English and Scottish Ballads*, Francis Child included ballad #188 *Archie O Cawfield* where he was taken prisoner and then broken out of jail. [5] Both ballads are very similar possibly indicating that the writer of *The Escape Of Old John Webb* was aware of the ballad *Archie O Cawfield*. Here is one of *Archie O Cawfield's* verses:

> I cannot work Billy, he says,
> I cannot work, Billy with thee,
> For fifteen stone of Spanish iron
> Lies fast to me with lock and key. [5]

The Escape Of Old John Webb

There were nine to guard the British ranks,
And five to guard the town about
And two to stand at either hand
And one to let old Tenor out.

There was eighty weight of good Spanish iron
Between his neck bone and his knee
But Billy took Johnny under his arm
And lugged him away right artfully.

Chorus: And Billy broke locks and Billy broke bolts
And Billy broke all that he came nigh,
Until he came to the dungeon door
And that he broke right manfully.

They mounted their horse and away did ride
And who but they rode gallantly
Until they came to the river bank
And there they alighted most merrily.

  Chorus: And Billy broke locks and Billy broke bolts
           And Billy broke all that he came nigh,
           Until he came to the dungeon door
           And that he broke right manfully.

And then they called for a room to dance
And who but they danced merrily
And the best dancer among them all
Was old John Webb, who was just set free.

  Chorus: And Billy broke locks and Billy broke bolts
           And Billy broke all that he came nigh,
           Until he came to the dungeon door
           And that he broke right manfully.

The British were comin' close on their heels
And who but they stood fearfully,
'Till Billy took Johnny up on his back
and carried him over it easily.

  Chorus: And Billy broke locks and Billy broke bolts
           And Billy broke all that he came nigh,
           Until he came to the dungeon door
           And that he broke right manfully.

TRADITIONAL – 1730 EVENT

The Charlestown Land Shark

The Charlestown Land Shark is a lament about a man imprisoned in a Salem for being a debtor. The ballad was found in the book *American Songs of Protest* by John Greenway and also in the Harris Broadside Collection at Brown University. Greenway states,

Photo of the original Old Salem Jail, 4 Federal Street, courtesy of Nancy Lutts

"In 1830, five out of six prisoners in New England and middle states jails were debtors, most of whom owed $20 or less." [7] Martin Van Buren introduced the first bill to the New York legislator in 1817 to completely repeal the law on debtor imprisonment. Colonel Richard M. Johnson, soon to be Vice President under Martin Van Buren, and himself a former debtor, introduced another bill in 1823 in the United States Senate to repeal the debtor's law. The law was abolished in 1832 and every state followed suit.

Greenway adds, "The 1815 freedom from class law was still beyond the vision of one unfortunate soul whose note had been bought by a professional creditor." [7]

> The Charlestown Land Shark my Note he bought,
> For to make money as he thought;
> The debt must lose, the cost must pay
> Unless the Shark must run away.
>
> He's Like the Shark, amazing fierce,
> Such and Sharks may they be more scarce,
> A greater Shark may catch him too,
> Then he will have what is his due.
>
> Like the great Shark, sees to devour,
> All that army fall within his power,
> Austere, morose, and Savage too,
> All you who know, is this not true?
>
> His pay but once that will not do,
> He wants it twice, they say 'tis true;
> A viler wretch can there be found,
> If you search the world around?
>
> He likes hush money, as they say,
> Give him enough and he will stay,
> For a small sum he will not wait,
> Because his avarice is too great.
>
> He's avaricious as the grave,
> In that a portion he will have,
> I think no one will sigh or mourn,
> When to the grave this Shark is borne.

His unjust gain his soul will haunt,
No pleasure to him will it grant;
His guilty conscience will it sting,
Down to the grave Death will him bring.

On Negro Hill they say he goes,
Why is that for you may suppose,
Why does this Shark these Blacks disgrace,
A Blacker mind a frowning face.

Tis said he once was very sick,
In consequence of a bad trick,
A certain nurse of him took care,
And she let out the whole affair.

He boost he's rich-most wretched too,
What is there bad he will not do?
A vagabond I think he'll be,
The day will come when we shall see.

In human misery he delights,
He fiercely barks before he bites,
I sought compassion, one could fine,
Because there was none in his mind.

In dirty business he is seen,
His conduct is amazing mean,
His wickedness to be portray'd,
Volumes before you must be laid.

To gratify his wicked mind,
Many in jail have been confin'd,
Vile wretched Shark, must pine away,
His debts must lose, the cost must pay.

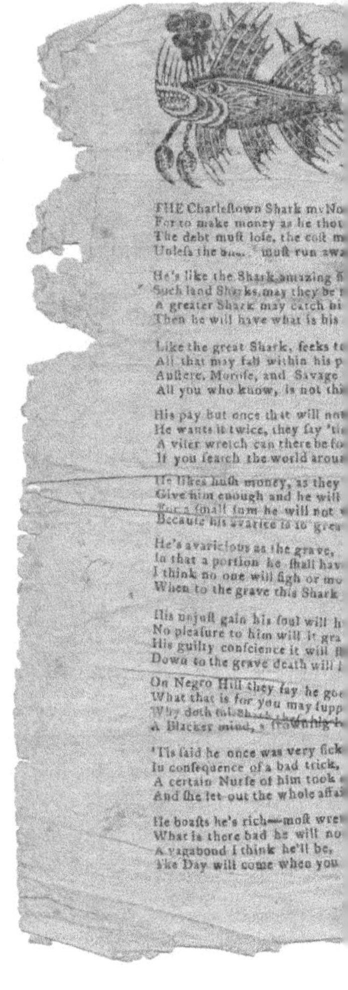

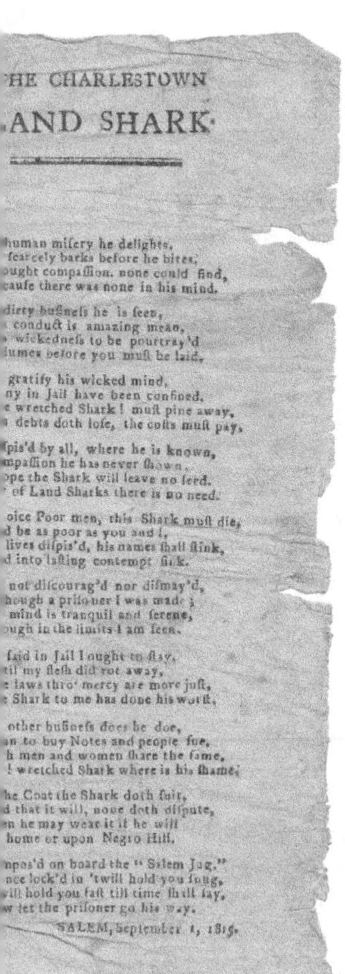

The Charlestown Land Shark, courtesy
of Harris Broadside Collection at the
John Hay Library, Brown University

Despis'd by all, where he is known,
Compassion he has never shown.
I hope the shark will leave no seed,
For of Land Sharks there is no need.

Rejoice, poor man, this Shark must die,
And be as poor as you and I,
He lives despis'd, his name shall stink,
And into the lasting contempt sink.

I'm not discouraged nor dismay'd,
Although a Prisoner I was made,
My mind is tranquil and serene,
Though in the limits I am seen.

He said in jail I ought to stay,
Until my flesh did rot away;
The laws tho' mercy are more just,
The Shark to me has done his worst

No other business does he doe,
Than to buy notes and people sue;
Both men and women share the same,
Ah! Wretched Shark! Where is his shame?

If the Coat the Shark doth suit,
And that it will, none doth dispute,
Then he may wear it if he will,
At home or upon Negro Hill.

Compos'd on board the "Salem Jug,"
If once lock'd in twill hold your snug;
'Twill hold you fast till time shall say,
Now let the Prisoner go his way.

TRADITIONAL – 1815

Susannah Martin

Susannah Martin, baptized Susannah North, was one of fourteen women executed during the Salem Witch Trials.

Lone Tree Hill in Amesbury, Massachusetts is a famous historical site that bore a tablet on its westerly side marking the site of George and Susannah Martin's home. The boulder has since been moved to make room for a highway and can be located on maps where the highway crosses Martin Road in Amesbury. [8]

The Witch House, courtesy of Mary Barker

John Allison sings *Susannah Martin* on the *Witches and War-Whoops: Early New England Ballads* LP. Diane Taraz, a local folk singer, also recorded the song on her CD called *A Silver Dagger ~ Exploring women's history through folk songs* in 2008.[9] Allison notes, "these ballads recount the sinister tragedy in the year 1692 when the childish fantasies of a handful of adolescent girls touched off a gruesome event—the Salem Witch Persecutions." [10] Allison has been collecting early New England ballads since the 1930s.. Of his collections, he states only two ballads have "know authorships" *The Death of Goody Nurse* by Rose Terry Cooke and *Flud Ireson* by John Greenleaf Whittier. [10] John Greenleaf Whittier also wrote *The Witch's Daughter* about Susannah Martin.

Let Goody Martin rest in peace,
I never knew her harm a fly,

And witch or not - God knows - not I?
I know who swore her life away;
And as God lives, I'd not condemn
An Indian dog on word of them.[11]

The LP also included the ballads: *The Gloucester Witch* or *Old Meg*, *Giles Corey* and *Old Mammy Redd*. Old Mammy Redd was an accused, elderly woman from Marblehead, Massachusetts. Allison also wrote on the back cover of his LP that his daughter, Joan Allison McGee, is a direct descendent of John Willard, who was one of the twenty executed on Gallows Hill in the Village of Salem. [10]

Susannah Martin

Susannah Martin was a witch who dwelt in Amesbury,
With brilliant eye and saucy tongue she worked her sorcery
And when into the judges court the sheriffs brought her hither,
The lilacs drooped as she passed by and then were seen to wither.

A witch she was, though trim and neat with comely head held high,
It did not seem that one as she with Satan so would vie
And when in court when the afflicted ones proclaimed her evil ways,
She laughed aloud and boldly then met Cotton Mather's gaze.

"Who hath bewitched these maids," he asked, and strong was her reply,
"If they be dealing in black arts, ye know as well as I"
And then the stricken ones made moan as she approached near,
They saw her shaped upon the beam so none could doubt 'twas there.

The neighbors 'round swore to the truth of her Satanic powers,
That she could fly o'er land, stream and come dry shod through showers
At night, twas said, she had appeared a cat of fearsome mien,
"Avoid she-devil," they had cried to keep their spirits clean.

The spectral evidence was weighed, then stern the parson spoke,
"Thou shalt not suffer a witch to live, tis written in the Book"
Susannah Martin so accused, spoke with flaming eyes,
"I scorn these things for they are naught but filthy gossips lies."

Now those bewitched, they cried her out, and loud their voice did ring,
They saw a bird above her head, an evil yellow thing
And so, beneath a summer sky, Susanna Martin died,
And still in scorn she faced the rope her comely head held high.

Susannah Martin was a witch who lived in Amesbury,
With brilliant eye and saucy tongue she worked her sorcery
And when into the judges court the sheriffs brought her hither,
The lilacs drooped as she passed by and then were seen to wither.

TRADITIONAL – UNKNOWN

A lecture and a song concerning the Robbery at Newbury to some men in jail at Salem

The Lecture and Song was printed for, and sold by, its author Jonathan Plummer. The song and lecture reveals that Plummer was selling his services for healing cancer and for the redemption of criminal acts. Levi and Laban Kenniston of Newmarket, NH were put in jail in Salem on suspicion of having robbed Major Goodrich of Newbury, Massachusetts on the nineteenth day of December 1816. Plummer states, "Three pieces of gold were found in the dwelling place of these Kenniston's, two of which were under a meat barrel in the cellar." Goodrich could identify one of the pieces of gold, "by the paper over it, and the figures marked on the back of it." [12]

The author states that it is not for him to judge these men, but is up to the Supreme Judicial Court. In the last verse of the song Plummer writes:

> And turn without the least delay,
> From every base and wicked way,
> That you salvation may obtain,
> And with my lovely Jesus reign.[12]

At the end of this article Plummer says, "Any person laboring under that dreadful malady a Cancer, by applying in good season to J. Plummer, the author of this lecture, may perhaps obtain a cure: the said Plummer having lately providentially made, a very important discovery, in regard to healing Cancers." [12]

*A lecture and a song concerning
the Robbery at Newbury to some men
in jail at Salem*

Unhappy brothers, friends in grief,
I come, I haste to your relief!
How can your inward fears be told?
Who can your dreadful state unfold?

If you have cruel robbers been,
You'll find some dreadful fruit of sin,
But if you're wrongfully accus'd,
I hope you'll not be much abus'd.

But whether you have robb'd or not,
It will be your quite certain lot,
Before my Jesus to appear,
There for your whole behavior here,

You'll surely have a trial rare,
A trial holy, just, and fair.
Oh! May you with the Saviour rise,
To blissful mansions in the skies.

When the last trumpet sounds aloud,
And wakes in graves the countless crowd,
When the old heav'ns blaze and roll,
And vanish like a burning scroll!

When all this globe will be on fire,
And earth and seas, in flames expire!
When he who on mount Calvary bled,
From death and hell, will call the dead!

And his holy angels come,
To endless joy his saints to doom,
And send his foes with grief to hell,
With Beelzebub the fool to dwell!

What guilt would then your bowels rend,
If you should find him not your friend!
And find yourself not friends to him,
But enemies in his esteem!

O for the sake of your poor souls,
Think while the present moment rolls,
Upon these all important things,
And honour much the kings of kings:

And turn without the least delay,
From every base and wicked way,
That you salvation may obtain,
And with my lovely Jesus reign.

JONATHAN PLUMMER – 1817

EMANCIPATION H[...]

Words by R.T.L.

M[...]

Introduction. *Moderato.*

~ 4 ~

Social Change

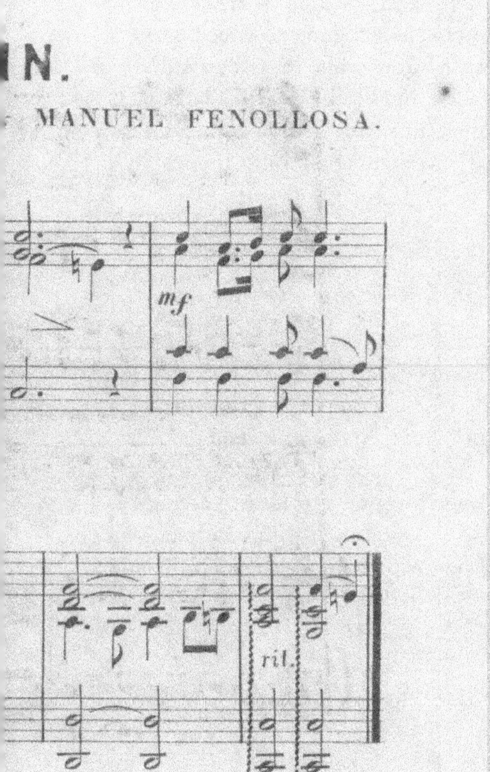

Emancipation Hymn

Manuel Fenollosa wrote the music for the *Emancipation Hymn* found at the Library of Congress. The *Emancipation Hymn* was published by Oliver Ditson & Co. and was "Composed and dedicated by permission to the Salem Union League" [1]

Manuel Fenollosa, a Spanish immigrant, came to Salem from Spain with his brother-in-law Manuel Emilio in 1838. *The Emancipation Hymn* was composed in 1863, and one year later Fenollosa held a concert in Salem celebrating Emancipation. Emilio and Fenollosa aided the famous 54th regiment, which was formed from white Massachusetts's officers and black recruits. The two immigrants were greatly influenced by their Salem abolitionist friends. [2]

The Civil War Statue in Greenlawn
Cemetery, courtesy of Mary Barker

Emancipation Hymn

Long our land in blood had weltered,
 Blood of dearest sons:
Long had Hero Spirits faltered,
 Not at booming guns:
Long our pray'r to Heav'n ascended,
 Fraught with bondmen's groans;
Long with victory's cheers had blended,
 Fettered manhood's moans!

God hath heard us, God hath heard us,
    And in mercy gives us bread for stones.
God hath heard us, God hath heard us,
    And in mercy gives us bread for stones.

Asking for a Land, for a Land united,
    We forgot the slave.
Pray'd we for our Country, for our Country blighted
    For our falling brave,
Left the bondman, chas'd by blood hounds,
    Scented thro' the cane,
God was with that panting brother;
    Pray'd we thus in vain!

    Ask, as we would serve another,
    Ask and he will hear again!
    Ask, as we would serve another,
    Ask and he will hear again!

He hath heard; O give Him glory!
    Heard the Bondman's pray'r:
O'er the warpath, red and glory
    Thro' the slave-hound's lair,
Peals the mandate of salvation,
    "Let my people go."
Humbled, bleeding, hear the nation,
    Answer, "Be it so!"

    Who shall weary! Who shall weary!
    Who shall falter! God is with us now!
    Who shall weary! Who shall weary!
    Who shall falter! God is with us now!

MANUEL FENOLLOSA AND R.T.L. – 1863

Get Off The Track

Get Off the Track was found in the Lester S. Levy Collection of Sheet Music at Johns Hopkins University. [3] The Hutchinson Family Singers had residences in New Hampshire and in Lynn, Massachusetts. They used their popularity in the 1840s to support a number of causes, including women's rights, utopian communities, and temperance. They also held a fierce opposition to slavery. [4] Jesse Hutchinson wrote this song to the tune of a lively dance tune that, at the time, was a popular minstrel melody written by Daniel Emmett called *Old Dan Tucker*.

Get Off the Track was also sung at the New England Anti-Slavery Convention held in Salem on April 11, 1844. [5] Hutchinson used the train to symbolize a "Liberator" coming down the rail as the "pro-slavery multitude were stupidly lingering on the track." [6]

Ho! The car, Emancipation,
Rides majestic thro' our nation;
Bearing on its train, the story,
Liberty! A nation's glory.

Roll it along! Roll it along!
Roll it along! Thro' the nation
Freedom's car, Emancipation

First of all the train, and greater,
Speeds the dauntless Liberator;
Onward cheered amid hosannas,
And the waving of free banners.

Roll it along! Roll it along!
Roll it along! Spread your banners
While the people shout hosannas.

Men of various predilections,
Frightened, run in all directions;
Merchants, editors, physicians,
Lawyers, priests and politicians.

Get out of the way! Get out of the way!
Get out of the way! Every station,
Clear the track of 'mancipation.

Let the ministers and churches,
Leave behind sectarian lurches;
Jump on board the car of freedom,
Ere it be too late to need them.

Sound the alarm! Sound the alarm!
Sound the alarm! Pulpit's thunder!
Ere too late, you see your blunder.

Politicians gazed, astounded,
When, at first our bell resounded;
Freight trains are coming, tell these foxes,
With our votes and ballot boxes.

Jump for your lives! Jump for your lives!
Jump for your lives! Politicians,
From your dangerous false positions.

Railroads to emancipation,
Cannot rest on Clay foundation;
And the tracks of 'The Magician',
Are but railroads to perdition.

Get Off the Track, courtesy of Lester S. Levy
Collection of Sheet Music, Sheridan Libraries,
Johns Hopkins University

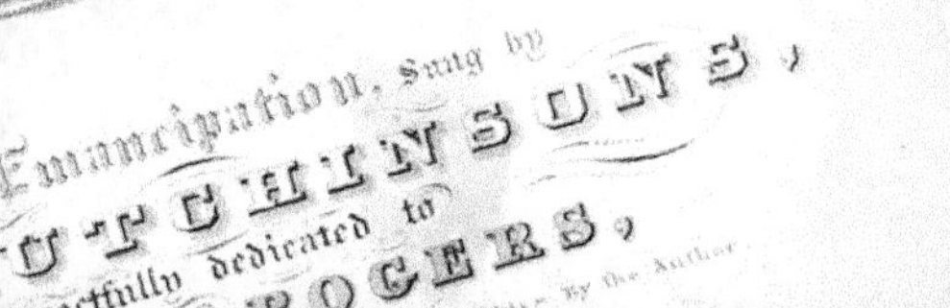

Pull up the rails! Pull up the rails!
Pull up the rails! Emancipation,
Cannot rest on such foundation.

All true friends of emancipation,
Haste to freedom's railroad station;
Quick into the cars get seated,
All is ready, and completed.

Put on the steam! Put on the steam!
Put on the steam! All are crying,
And the liberty flags are flying.

Now, again the bell is tolling,
Soon you'll see the car wheels rolling;
Hinder not their destination,
Chartered for emancipation.

Wood up the fire! Wood up the fire!
Wood up the fire! Keep it flashing,
While the train goes onward dashing.

Hear the mighty car wheels humming!
Now look out! The engine's coming!
Church and statesmen! Hear the thunder!
Clear the track! Or you'll fall under.

Get off the track! Get off the track!
Get off the track! All are singing,
While the liberty bell is ringing.

The Hutchinson Family Singers at Tabernacle
Chapel in Salem, courtesy of Ann Lewis
Women's Suffrage Collection

On triumphant, see them bearing,
Through sectarian rubbish tearing;
Th' bell and whistle and the steaming,
Startles thousands from their dreaming.

Look out for the cars! Look out for the cars!
Look out for the cars! While the bell rings,
Ere the sound your funeral knell rings.

See the people run to meet us;
At the depots thousands greet us;
All take seats with exultation,
In the car, Emancipation.

Huzza! Huzza! Huzza! Huzza!
Huzza! Huzza! Emancipation,
Soon will bless our happy nation.
Huzza! Huzza! Huzza!

JESSE HUTCHINSON – 1844

The Famous Old Time
HUTCHINSON FAMILY
"TRIBES OF JOHN and JESSE."
——AT THE——
TABERNACLE CHAPEL, SALEM,
MONDAY EVENING, FEB. 26, 1883.

Tickets 25 cents, for sale at the Door, and at Wm. H. Kehew's, at
Lowery's Art Store, 116 Washington St.

Concert begins Promptly at Quarter of Eight o'clock.

CHARACTERISTIC CONCERTS.

No company of Singers in the world has given as much pleasure, or been so well patronized by all classes of the community, for their songs are full of joyful sentiment, of Hope and Good-will, and are always rendered in an earnest, spirited manner, and the American people as well as the European have appreciated and applauded them, while humanity has been elevated to a higher standard of civilization.

PROGRAM.

QUARTET.   "We're with you once again, kinds friends."   *Hutchinson*

0 Thou To Whom in Ancient Time

John Pierpont wrote *0 Thou To Whom in Ancient Time* [7] for the opening of the Independent Congregational Church at Barton Square in Salem, Massachusetts, on December 7, 1824. Pierpont was born in 1785 in Litchfield, Connecticut and was the appointed pastor of the Hollis Street Church in Boston from 1819 – 1845. His poetry was often read at antislavery and temperance meetings.

On April 24 1899 the Independent Congregational Church united with the East Church Society and the Second Church to form one corporation called the Second Church. Services were held at the Second Church in Washington Square (now the Salem Witch Museum) with Pastor Alfred of Manchester. [8] The original location of the Independent Congregational church building is now a bank parking lot.

Charles Cleveland who arranged and edited the *American Literature with Biographical Sketches and Selections From Their Works; A compendium of American literature* where the text was discovered, was born on December 3, 1802 in Salem and graduated from Dartmouth College in 1827. [9]

0 Thou to whom in ancient time
The lyre of Hebrew bards was strung
Whom kings adored in song sublime
And prophets praised with glowing tongue

Not now on Zion's height alone
Thy favor'd worshipper may dwell
Nor where at sultry noon thy Son
Sat weary by the Patriarch's well

From every place below the skies
The grateful song the fervent prayer
The incense of the heart may rise
To heaven and find acceptance there

In this thy house whose doors we now
For social worship first unfold
To thee the suppliant throng shall bow
While circling years on years are roll 'd

To thee shall Age with snowy hair
And Strength and Beauty bend the knee
And Childhood lisp with reverent air
Its praises and its prayers to thee

O thou to whom in ancient time
The lyre of prophet bards was strung
To thee at last in every clime
Shall temples rise and praise be sung

DR. JOHN PIEPONT – 1824

A Parting Hymn

Charlotte Louise Bridges Forten Grimké (1837 – 1914) was an African American, anti-slavery activist, poet, and educator. In 1854 Forten joined the household of Amy Matilda Cassey and her second husband Charles Lenox Remond in Salem where she attended the Higginson Grammar School, a private academy for young women. [10] She was the only non-white student in a class of 200. After graduating, Forten studied literature and teaching at the Salem Normal School (Now Salem Sate University). Her first teaching position was at the former Eppes Grammar School in Salem. She became the first African American hired to teach white students in a Salem public school in 1856. [11] *The Massachusetts Teacher and Journal of Home and School Education, Volume 9* published Forten's poem *A Parting Blessing* or *A Parting Hymn* stating that the poem is a "specimen of the beauty, pure, and philanthropic sentiment, lofty aspiration, and of sublime faith." [12]

A Parting Hymn

When winter's royal robes of white
From hill and vale are gone,
And the glad voices of the spring
Upon the air are borne,
Friends, who have met with us before,
Within these walls shall meet no more.

Forth to a noble work they go:
O, may their hearts keep pure,
And hopeful zeal and strength be theirs

To labor and endure,
That they an earnest faith may prove
By words of truth and deeds of love.

May those, whose holy task it is
To guide impulsive youth,
Fail not to cherish in their souls
A reverence for truth;
For teachings which the lips impart
Must have their source within the heart.

May all who suffer share their love --
The poor and the oppressed;
So shall the blessing of our God
Upon their labors rest.
And may we meet again where all
Are blest and freed from every thrall.

CHARLOTTE L. FORTEN GRIMKE – 1854

Forten also became a member of the Salem Female Anti-Slavery Society (formed 1832) where she was involved in coalition building and fund-raising. She proved to be an influential activist and leader of civil rights.

Musical Entertainment

at Mechanic Hall, Salem

This concert, led by Salem resident Manuel Fenollosa, was held at Mechanic Hall in Salem on January 6, 1863 for the benefit of the sick and wounded Massachusetts soldiers that fought in the Civil War. [13] Hattie Safford, E. W. Silsbee, J. F. Tuckerman and E. H. Randall of Salem, E. T. Kemble of Beverly, and M. C. Upton of Danvers performed at the concert. The program was a combination of classical pieces with the singing of two newly composed parlor ballads *Her Bright Smile Haunts Me Still,* and *Goodbye, Sweet Heart.*

The song, *Her Bright Smile Haunts Me Still* was written by W. T. Wrighton and J. E. Carpenter, and was originally published in 1857. Recently, the song has had renewed interest through the folk process after being published in *Traditional American Folk Songs* from the Anne and Frank Warner Collection. [14] This program could be one of the first documented times that *Her Bright Smile Haunts Me Still* was performed.

For the Sick and Wounded
MASSACHUSETTS SOLDIERS.

AMATEUR CONCERT
IN AID OF THE
NEW ENGLAND WOMEN'S
Auxiliary Sanitary Commission.

MANUEL FENOLLOSA

takes great pleasure in announcing to the public, that with the co-operation of the following Ladies and Gentlemen, who have most kindly consented to take part, he will
REPEAT HIS
MUSICAL ENTERTAINMENT,
AT MECHANIC HALL, SALEM,
ON TUESDAY, JANUARY 6, 1863,
the net proceeds of which will be handed to the above Association, to enable it to continue the good work of helping the sick and wounded defenders of their country.

MRS. E. T. KEMBLE, of Beverly.
MRS. M. C. UPTON, of S. Danvers.
MISS HATTIE SAFFORD,
MISS E. W. SILSBEE,
DR. J. F. TUCKERMAN,   of Salem.
MR. E. H. RANDALL.

TICKETS, AT 25 CENTS EACH,
may be obtained at all the Bookstores in the City, and at the Door, on the evening of the Concert.

DOORS OPEN AT 6 1-2 O'CLOCK. PERFORMANCES AT 7 1-2.

CHARLES W. SWASEY, PRINTER, No. 27 WASHINGTON STREET, SALEM.

New England Women's Auxiliary Sanitary Commission Program Booklet, courtesy of Christine Elizabeth Mistretta's private collection.

The Cornerstone Hymn

The Cornerstone Hymn was written by Hosea Ballou and was first sung on August 17, 1808 when the First Universalist laid a cornerstone to mark the place where their new building was to be raised. Benjamin Ward donated a plot of land to the church Trustees on January 22, 1806, so that a building could be erected for the Universalist Society of Salem. The lot valued at one thousand dollars was located on St. Peter Street. However, the neighborhood, at that time, was considered undesirable since St. Peter's Street was also known as "Prison Lane" because the county jail was situated in the immediate vicinity. [15]

The Cornerstone Hymn was again sung at the celebration concert for the First Universalist Society's 200th birthday. The earliest gathering of the First Universalist Society was Christmas Eve 1805 in a living room on Lynde Street. According to Sarah Smith, some 200 years later a concert featuring a small orchestra portrayed "the musical history of the church." Sarah, who was a Salem resident and long time church member, noted that many of their hymns reflected Universalist themes for social change like abolitionism, anti-war activism, and women's suffrage. [16] Bill Smith, Sarah's husband, put these lyrics to a new melody.

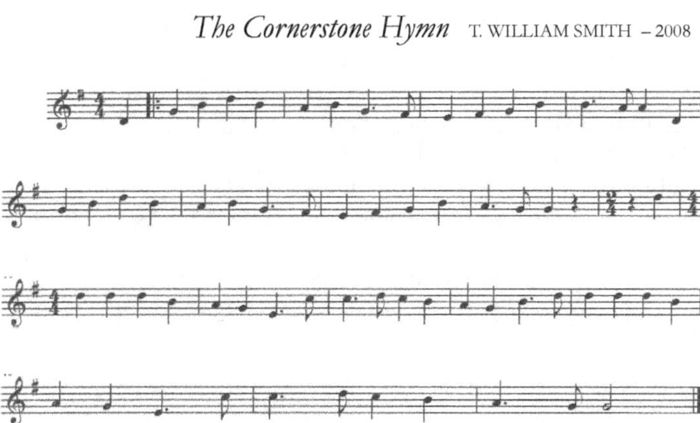

The Cornerstone Hymn   T. WILLIAM SMITH – 2008

The Cornerstone Hymn

On Salem's fair and pleasant shore,
Thy church, O Lord, in mercy meet;
Display thy grace, display thy pow'r,
And show the impress of thy feet.

   Chorus: Oil this well tri'd chief corner stone
      Shall rise to thee a sacred dome.

Here, on the margin of the tide,
By thy rich goodness, long shall stand;
Its spacious walls, extended wide,
And speak the favour of thy hand.

   Chorus: Oil this well tri'd chief corner stone,
      Shall rise to thee a sacred dome.

May lib'ral souls, who feel thy grace,
Build here, in honour of thy name,
And join to consecrate the place,
Thy cause and honour to maintain.

   Chorus: Oil this well tri'd chief corner stone,
      Shall rise to thee a sacred dome.

Yea, from their rich, abundant store,
May each to thee an off'ring bring,
And from the horn of plenty pour,
Oblations to their heav'nly King.

   Chorus: Oil this well tri'd chief corner stone,
      Shall rise to thee a sacred dome.

In honor of their Saviour's name,
May Salem's sons and daughters join,
To raise thin Temple to thy fame,
Their heart in truth and love combine.

> Chorus: Oil this well tri'd chief corner stone,
> Shall rise to thee a sacred dome.

As Isra'l, in the days of old,
To build thine house, rich offerings made,
Of iron, silver, brass and gold,
No be our willing gifts display'd.

> Chorus: Oil this well tri'd chief corner stone,
> Shall rise to thee a sacred dome.

Succeed our labor and our cost;
Sustain with strength each workman's arm;
Let the fair prospect not be lost;
Preserve from accident and harm.

> Chorus: Oil this well tri'd chief corner stone,
> Shall rise to thee a sacred dome.

May all who love the Lord rejoice,
To see these spacious walls ascend;
And join with heart, and soul, and voice,
To praise their Saviour and their friend.

> Chorus: Oil this well tri'd chief corner stone,
> Shall rise to thee a sacred dome.

HOSEA BALLOU – 1808
T. WILLIAM SMITH – 2008

BOSTON JOURNAL OF SHEET MUSIC.
No. 123.   January 19,   1905.
Published Weekly.   Subscription, $2.00 per year.

RICHMOND MARCH

Composed and Dedicated to

Capt. THOS. J.

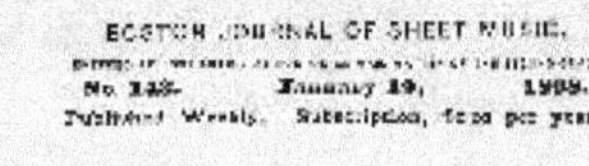

BY JEAN M. MISSUD

Conductor of the SALEM CADET BAND

~ 5 ~
Conflict

Departure of the Salem Light Infantry

Departure of the Salem Light Infantry was found in the Harris Broadsides Collection at Brown University. [1] The Salem City Guards 7th Massachusetts Volunteer Militia; Company H was accepted into state service on April 19, 1861. They left Salem and arrived at Faneuil Hall in Boston on April 20, 1861. [2] According to the *Salem Register*, the Mechanic Light Infantry led by Captain Pierson and the Salem City Guards led by Captain Danforth were ordered to join Commander Colonel Lawrence's regiment. The Mechanic Light Infantry numbered 110 men and the Salem City Guards 64. [3]

To arms! To Arms! Our country calls;
The Salem Infantry reply,
And quickly; leave their armory halls,
To make the Southern rebels fly.

A company of fearless men,
In all their youthful strength and force,
'Mid cheers and shouting take the train,
That bears them on their course.

There's one on whom we can confide,
On him implicitly rely;
His honor needs not to be tried,
Temptation he can well defy.

A frame with all the force of youth,
A mind from folly's shackles clear,
A heart of love, and hope, and truth;
Our Willie's one whom all revere.

Departure of the Salem Light Infantry,
courtesy of Harris Broadside Collection
at the John Hay Library, Brown University

His father's pride his mother's joy,
A brother true, a faithful friend-
May God protect this noble boy,
In safety to his home to send.

And sad was Charlie Dimon's face,
But duty was his polar guide;
And so with trust he took his place,
And ranked himself on Union's side.

May he in Willie's friendship find,
A balm to sooth the homesick heart;
And may they both forever mind,
That's good advice, "Act well your part."

Among the troops was one bright face,
That gleamed with patriotic zeal;
And nobly handsome, full of grace,
On his pure brow is stamped truth's seal.

The love of country burns within,
The soul that's large with love for all,
And Johnnie Lakeman deemed in sin
To answer not his country's call.

Oh! Sad hearts they leave behind-
And tearful faces, daily met,
Do tell full well that ties that bind,
We never, never can forget.

"The pride of Salem" – they have gone,
To battle for their native land;
God grant that they may soon return,
In safety, and unbroken band.

S.J.C.N. APRIL 19TH – 1861

Lines written for the

Second Reunion of the 23rd Regiment

These lines were discovered in the Broadside Collection at the Center for Popular Music at Middle Tennessee State University. Charles Henry Webber wrote the song in 1872. He said that the 23rd Regiment was composed of six companies from Essex County, and one each from Bristol, Plymouth, Middlesex, and Worcester counties. The companies were assembled in Lynnfield, Massachusetts, on September 28, 1861, though some of the men were not mustered until December 5 after the regiment's arrival in Annapolis, Maryland. [4] Ten years after their first muster, the surviving soldiers gathered for a reunion in Salem, Massachusetts and formed the 23rd Regiment Association. The broadside was read at this event. [5]

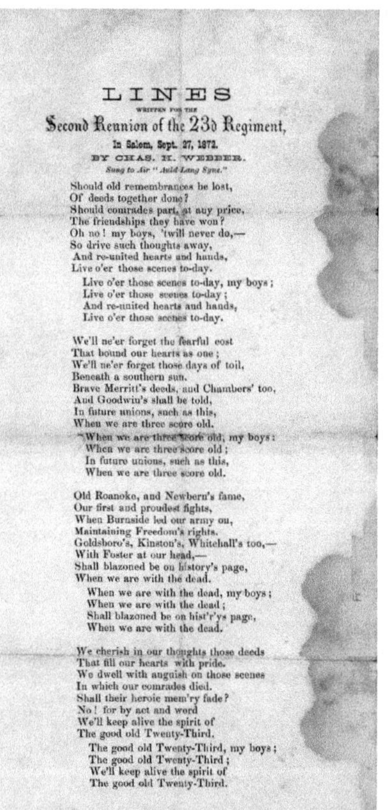

Second Reunion of the 23rd Regiment, courtesy of the Kenneth S. Goldstein Collection of American Song Broadsides Center for Popular Music, Middle Tennessee State University

On September 28, 1905, the Association dedicated a bronze plaque set in a 58-ton boulder, commemorating the service of the 23rd Regiment Massachusetts Volunteer Infantry during the Civil War from 1861 - 1865. [5] The memorial stands on Winter Street near the Salem Commons.

Should old remembrances be lost
Of deeds together done?
Should comrades part, at any price,
The friendship they have won?

Oh no! My boys, 'twill never do,
So drive such thoughts away,
And reunited hearts and hands,
Live o'ver those scenes to-day.

Live o'er those scenes today, my boys,
Live o'er those scenes today,
And re-united hearts and hands,
Live o'ver those scenes to-day.

We'll ne'er forget the fearful cost,
That bound our hearts as one,
We'll ne'er forget those days of toil,
Beneath the southern sun.

Brave Merritt's deeds, and Chamber's too,
And Goodwin's shall be told,
In future unions, such as this,
When we are three score old.

When we are three score old, my boys,
When we are three score old,

Boulder Commemorating the Service of the 23rd Regiment Salem, Massachusetts, Postcard courtesy of Sal Pangallo

In future unions, such as this,
When we are three score old,

Old Roanoke, and Newbern's fame,
Our first and proudest fights,
When Burnside led our army on,
Maintaining Freedom's rights.

Goldboro's, Kinston's Whitehall's too,-
With Foster at our head,-
Shall blazoned be on history's page,
When we are with the dead.

When we are with the dead, my boys;
When we are with the dead;
Shall blazoned be on history's page,
When we are with the dead.

We cherish in our thoughts and deeds
That fill our hearts with pride.
We dwell with anguish on those scenes
In which our comrades died.

Shall their heroic mem'ry fade?
No! for by act and word
We'll keep alive the spirit of
The good old Twenty-third.

The good old Twenty-third, my boys;
The good old Twenty-third;
We'll keep alive the spirit of,
The good old Twenty-third.

CHARLES HENRY WEBBER – 1872

When Johnny Comes Marching Home

Marwood Darlington author of *Irish Orpheus, The Life of Patrick S. Gilmore Bandmaster Extraordinary* states that Patrick Gilmore, at age 27, left the Boston Brigade Band to lead the Salem Band. Under his leadership, the Salem Band became one of the "finest bands in New England." [6]

Gilmore wrote *When Johnny Comes Marching Home* under the pseudonym of Louis Lambert to celebrate a soldier returning home from the Civil War. "It was inspired by the Battle of Gettysburg in July 1863 when the tide of the American Civil War began to turn in favor of the Union." [7] According to Margaret Bradford Boni, who wrote and compiled the *Fireside Book of Folk Songs*, Gilmore could have heard this tune when it was sung by an "African American," but as Boni pointed out, since Gilmore was an Irishman, it is more likely that the tune had Irish roots. [8] Louis Elson, writer of *The National Music of America and its Sources*, states that *Johnny Comes Marching Home* has a similar melody to the Irish songs *John Anderson, My Jo,* [9] and *Johnny, I Hardly Knew Ye*, an Irish protest song.

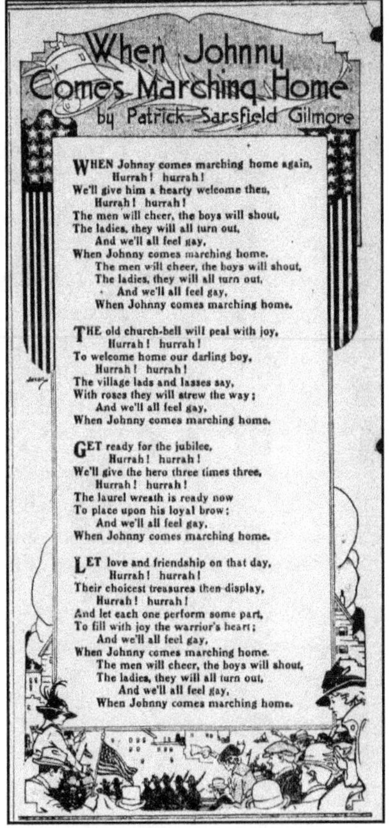

When Johnny Comes Marching Home - Broadside, courtesy of Jarlath MacNamara

As stated on the Library of Congress website, "It is possible that this air was written before Gilmore's *When Johnny Comes Marching Home* and that Gilmore unconsciously borrowed from the tune from an African-American spiritual." [10] To this day there is on-going discussion about the origins of this song.

When Johnny Comes Marching Home

When Johnny comes marching home again
    Hurrah! Hurrah!
We'll give him a hearty welcome then
    Hurrah! Hurrah!
The men will cheer and the boys will shout
    The ladies they will all turn out
And we'll all feel gay
    When Johnny comes marching home.
And we'll all feel gay
    When Johnny comes marching home.

The old church bell will peal with joy
    Hurrah! Hurrah!
To welcome home our darling boy,
    Hurrah! Hurrah!
The village lads and lassies say
    With roses they will strew the way,
And we'll all feel gay
    When Johnny comes marching home.
And we'll all feel gay
    When Johnny comes marching home.

Get ready for the Jubilee,
　　　　Hurrah! Hurrah!
We'll give the hero three times three,
　　　　Hurrah! Hurrah!
The laurel wreath is ready now
　　　　To place upon his loyal brow
And we'll all feel gay
　　　　When Johnny comes marching home.
And we'll all feel gay
　　　　When Johnny comes marching home.

Let love and friendship on that day,
　　　　Hurrah, hurrah!
Their choicest pleasures then display,
　　　　Hurrah, hurrah!
And let each one perform some part,
　　　　To fill with joy the warrior's heart,
And we'll all feel gay
　　　　When Johnny comes marching home.
And we'll all feel gay
　　　　When Johnny comes marching home.

Additional lyrics

In eighteen hundred and sixty-one
　　　　Hurrah! Hurrah!
That was when the war begun,
　　　　Hurrah! Hurrah!
In eighteen hundred and sixty-two,
　　　　Both sides were falling to,
And we'll all drink stone wine,
　　　　When Johnny comes marching home.
And we'll all drink stone wine,
　　　　When Johnny comes marching home.

GRAND CONCERT

BY

Gilmore's Salem Brass Band,

Monday Evening, February 16, 1857.

PROGRAMME.

PART I.

1—Overture, "Fra Diavolo,".............................Auber

2—Obligato

3—Divertise

4—Two Pie
No. 1—So
No. 2—Ne

5—Solo for E

6—Grand D
Mr

7—Marien

8—Scotch M

9—Trumpet

10—Pot Pour

11—Quadrille

12—Anvil Ch

13—Battle Ga

14—Grand F
Dedicated to t

Doors open at

Times Job Office—

In eighteen hundred and sixty-three,
    Hurrah! Hurrah!
Old Abe, he ended slavery
    Hurrah! Hurrah!
In eighteen hundred and sixty-three
    Old Abe, he ended slavery
And we'll all drink stone wine,
    When Johnny comes marching home.
And we'll all drink stone wine,
    When Johnny comes marching home.

In eighteen hundred and sixty-four,
    Hurrah! Hurrah!
Abe called for five hundred thousand more,
    Hurrah! Hurrah!
In eighteen hundred and sixty-five,
    They talked rebellion--strife;
And we'll all drink stone wine
    When Johnny comes marching home.
And we'll all drink stone wine,
    When Johnny comes marching home.

Grand Concert - Gilmore's
Salem Brass Band, courtesy
of Jarlath MacNamara

PATRICK GILMORE AKA LOUIS LAMBERT – 1863

Down on Manila's Bay

Down on Manila's Bay is courtesy of Historic Beverly The song is sung to the tune of *Auld Lang Syne* and dedicated to the United Spanish War Veterans of America in honor of their 50th Anniversary and to Congressional Medal of Honor recipient, Salem's own John P. Riley. [11]

Riley is the only Salem resident to receive the Congressional Medal of Honor. According to the *Salem Evening News* dated September 2, 1898, he received the honor on May 11, 1898. Riley was one of the crew of the gunboat, *Nashville*, during the Spanish American War. He and several volunteers severed a cable linking communication between Cuba and Spain. [12]

A large boulder engraved with his name and surrounded by flagpoles defines the perimeter of Riley's monument near the Salem Post Office. The dedication took place on June 7, 1959. Riley lived at 3 Warner Street in Salem, working as a city employee until his retirement in 1944. Riley died on November 16, 1950 and is buried at Greenlawn Cemetery. [13]

'Twas back in 1898; down on Manila's Bay;
When Comrades true; in Navy Blue; volunteered that day-
To leave their Battleship of War; to defend a Flag so grand
To cut the Enemy's Cable; separating Manilas' Mainland.

No questions comrade did you have to ask; no answers to explain;
For revenge was there in every heart; for the sinking of the Maine.
Men stepped forward for the task; in silence; and devotion
Looking only back; at the Union Jack; the pride of America's Ocean.

You came forward with the others; without hesitation or fear;
With hooks; knifes; and cutters; brave men abreast; rowed near-
Amid the two sides of the enemy; you found their cabled wire-
And cut it to hell in pieces; as the enemy opened fire.

UNKNOWN – 1948

Ode of War and Washington

Ode of War and Washington was written during the American Revolution by Salem born Jonathan M. Sewall and sung to the tune of *The British Grenadiers*. Sewall studied at Harvard College, entered into the mercantile business, and eventually settled in Portsmouth, New Hampshire where he "passed the remainder of his life, with a high character for integrity." [11] He died March 29, 1808 at the age of 60. [14]

According to Samuel Kettell, editor of *Specimens of American Poetry*, the *Ode of War and Washington* was a patriotic song, which "was sung throughout the country during the revolutionary war and served to inspire zeal and courage in the cause for independence." [15]

From an article found in the *Salem Mercury* dated October 27, 1789:

> The President of the United States is expected to honor this town with a visit on Thursday next, about noon. We are informed that he will come by the way of Marblehead--that he will tarry in this town one night, and continue his tour eastward the next morning. From the judicious choice made by the inhabitants of this town of committee for addressing the President, and for making arrangements for his reception, we venture to predict, that he will be received here in style becoming the rank of the town, and coinciding with the ardent love and affection while every son and daughter of Salem bears this amiable and illustrious perusing. [16]

The war for independence ended and George Washington became president. Washington traveled throughout the colonies. On October 29, 1789 he visited Salem to review the troupes and attend a ball at the Assembly House. He spent the evening at the private residence of Joshua Ward, a shipping master and rum distiller. [17] The house is located on 148 Washington Street and is now a small boutique hotel called The Merchant.

The Joshua Ward House, courtesy of Mary Barker

Ode of War and Washington

Vain Britons, boast no longer, with fine indignity,
Your valiant marching legions, your matchless strength at sea.
For we, your loyal sons oppressed, have girded our swords on.
    Huzza! Huzza! Huzza! For War and Washington!

Urged on by North and vengeance, those valiant champions came,
Loud bellowing Tea and Treason, and George was all on flame,
Yet sacrilegious as it seems, we rebels still live on,
    And laugh at all their empty puffs,—huzza for Washington!

Still deaf to mild entreaties, still blind to England's good,
You have for thirty pieces, betray'd your country's blood.
Like Aesop's greedy cur, you'll gain a shadow for your bone,
    Yet find us fearful shades indeed, inspired by Washington!

Mysterious! Unexampled! Incomprehensible!
The blundering schemes of Britain, their folly, pride, and zeal.
Like lions how ye growl and threat! mere asses have you shown,
    And ye shall share an ass's fate, and drudge for Washington!

Your dark, unfathom'd counsels, our weakest heads defeat,
Our children rout your armies, our boats destroy your fleet,
And to complete the dire disgrace, coop'd up within a town,
    You live, the scorn of all our host, the slaves of Washington!

Great heaven! is this the nation, whose thundering arms were hurl'd,
Through Europe, Africa, India? whose navy ruled a world?
The lustre of your former deeds, whole ages of renown,
    Lost in a moment, or transferred to us and Washington!

Yet think not thirst of glory, unsheathes our vengeful swords,
To rend your bands asunder, and cast away your cords.
'T is heaven-born freedom fires us all, and strengthens each brave son,
    From him who humbly guides the plough, to godlike Washington!

For this, Oh could our wishes, your ancient rage inspire,
Your armies should be doubled, in numbers, force, and fire.
Then might the glorious conflict prove which best deserved the boon,
    America or Albion; a George, or Washington!

Fired with the great idea, our fathers' shades would rise;
To view the stern contention, the gods desert their skies.
And Wolfe; 'mid hosts of heroes, superior bending down,
    Cry out with eager transport, God save great Washington!

Should George, too choice of Britons, to foreign realms apply?
And madly arm half Europe, yet still we would defy
Turk, Hessian, Jew, and Infidel, or all those powers in one,
    While Adams guides our senate, our camp great Washington!

Should warlike weapons fail us, disdaining slavish fears,
To swords we'll beat our ploughshares, our pruning hooks to spears,
And rush, all desperate! On our foe, nor breathe till battle won;
    Then shout, and shout America! And conquering Washington!

Proud France should view with terror, and haughty Spain revere,
While every warlike nation would court alliance here.
And George, his minions trembling round, dismounting from his throne,
    Pay homage to America, and glorious Washington!

JONATHAN M. SEWALL – 1789

Americans to Arms

Americans To Arms is sung to the tune *Britons To Arms* and was printed as a broadside in Salem, Massachusetts, in 1775. [18]

AMERICA's Sons, yourselves prepare
For LIBERTY now calls for War.
Exert yourselves with Force and Might,
Show how AMERICANS can fight,
And only to maintain their Right Farewell England.

Rouse, rouse, my Boys, 'tis FREEDOM that calls;
Mount, mount your Guns, prepare your Ball;
We'll fight, we'll conquer, or we'll die,
But we'll maintain our LIBERTY,
And hand it to Posterity Farewell England.

Hark! From afar, how the Trumpet sounds,
See the bold Heroes in Blood and Wounds;
Drums a-beating, Colors flying,
Cannons roaring, brave Men dying,
Such are the bold AMERICANS Farewell England.

AMERICA, which rules over the Land,
Her valiant Sons join Hand in Hand;
United Sons of FREEDOM may
Drive all those Dogs of War away,
With Triumph crown AMERICA Farewell England.

Why then should we be daunted at all,
Since we've engag'd in so noble a Call?
As fighting for our CHURCH and LAWS,
And dying in so just a CAUSE, '
'Twill prove the fatal Overthrow Of Old England.

E. RUSSELL – 1775

Salem Mechanick Infantry Quick Step

The Salem Mechanick Infantry Quick Step [19] was found in the Lester S. Levy Collection of Sheet Music. The tune was written and arranged by John Holloway and published by Ives & Putman in Salem. The Boston Brass Band played the tune for the first time on October 13, 1836 on the 29th anniversary of the Salem Mechanick Light Infantry.

Salem Mechanick Infantry Quick Step, courtesy of Lester S. Levy Collection of Sheet Music, Sheridan Libraries, Johns Hopkins University

Salem Independent Cadet Quick Step, courtesy of Lester S. Levy Collection of Sheet Music, Sheridan Libraries, Johns Hopkins University

Salem Independent Cadet Quick Step

The Salem Independent Cadet Quick Step [20] was found in the Lester S. Levy Collection of Sheet Music. The tune was dedicated to Captain S. B. Foster and the officers and members of the Division Corps of Independent Cadets at their fall parade on October 17, 1848. The piece was composed by Zetzsche, arranged by S. Knaebel, and performed at the parade by the Flagg's Boston Brass Band.

Original Ode,
The First Shot of Freedom

Original Ode, The First Shot of Freedom was composed by Miss L.L.A. Very and was sung on the morning of the Memorial Services at the Centennial Anniversary of Leslie's Expedition to Salem, on Friday February 26, 1875.[21] This confrontation known as Leslie's Retreat occurred on February 26, 1775. The British troops led by Lt. Colonel Alexander Leslie, left Marblehead and arrived in Salem at the North Bridge. The citizens of Salem successfully resisted the advancement of British soldiers, without firing a shot:

> This move of the British army was the first open
> invasion of the rights and freedom of the people
> and brought out in broad daylight the first actual
> resistance in arms to the Royal authority of the
> crown. [21]

The musical program at the service was under the direction of Salem resident, Mr. Manuel Fenollosa. He wrote the *Emancipation Hymn* in 1863 and the singing was by a choir selected from the Salem Oratorio Society.

Original Ode, The First Shot of Freedom

Leslie's Retreat, sounding far through the years!
Their footsteps are marching, marching today;
Gone are the trials privations and fears
Our ancestors bore 'neath England's proud sway.
Sown in War's furrows with blood and with tears,
The harvest of Peace we are reaping today.

Chorus: The first shot of Freedom today we repeat!
        Here's to the memory of Leslie's Retreat!
        A health to the brave ones of old!

Back from our borders by land and by sea,
Born unto freedom we turn back the feet,
Feet of oppressors who e'er they may be,
They'll march to the tune of Leslie's Retreat!
Back from our borders by land and by sea,
We turn back oppressors who e'er they may be.

Chorus: The first shot of Freedom today we repeat!
        Here's to the memory of Leslie's Retreat!
        A health to the brave ones of old!

Between wrong and right let us e'er draw the line,
Though poverty s here there red coats so fine;
When Georges send down their mandates so wise,
Our North Bridge shall rival the famed Bridge of Sighs.
Cherish the names of the brave and the true,
Barnard and Sprague and Pickering too.

Chorus: The first shot of Freedom today we repeat!
        Here's to the memory of Leslie's Retreat!
        A health to the brave ones of old!

MISS L. L. A. VERY – 1875

Original Ode

Dr. John P. Ordway was born in Salem in 1824 and wrote *The Original Ode* in 1869. *The Original Ode* was sung on June 6, 1870 at the two hundred and thirty-second anniversary of the Ancient and Honorable Artillery Company. [22] According to Oliver Ayer Roberts, author of the book *History of The Military Company of the Massachusetts,* at ten o' clock in the morning, the Company stood in front of Faneuil Hall and marched to the State House. Patrick S. Gilmore's band marched at the head of the parade. Upon arriving at the State House, Governor Claflin, his staff, and other invited guests were received with the "customary formalities" and were then escorted through the streets of Boston beginning at Park Street and ending at the Old South Church where annual religious exercises of the corps were held. [22] Reverend W.H.H. Murray of Boston conducted the services and delivered a sermon. After the prayer, *The Original Ode* was sung.

Once more we meet as soldiers true,
The bond of union o'er us;
With heart and hand we strike anew,
For Liberty to shield us.

This is the day and this the hour
When brothers meet in kindness;
For no foe shall strike
From the freeman's tower
The Flag that still shines in brightness.

That peace may reign each loyal heart
Prays for its folds to compass;
Through hill and dale with playful art,
The joyful anthem round us.

In ancient times our ranks were lined,
With men who knew that glory
Was to be brave their hearts enshrined,
With us repeat the story.

This is the day and this the hour
When brothers meet in kindness;
For no foe shall strike
From the freeman's tower
The Flag that still shines in brightness.

Then gather round with hearts profound,
Almighty aid imploring -
Tune well each voice with sweetest sound,
T1l all above seem soaring.

This is the day and this the hour,
When brothers meet in kindness;
For no foe shall strike
From the freeman's tower
The Flag that still shines in brightness.

DR. JOHN P. ORDWAY – 1869

Song of the Minute Man

Song of the Minute Man was discovered in the Harris Broadside Collection at the John Hay Library at Brown University. [23] There is also a copy in the Frederick E. Berry Library at Salem State University. *Song of the Minute Man* was originally written on March 13, 1777 by a Mr. Boundbruck. The phonetically spelled text was copied and then published. This version was taken from a manuscript that was in the possession of local businessman George R. Curwen, Esquire The broadside was sold by the Antique Relics & Company at an exhibition held by the Ladies' Centennial Committee of Salem on December 15, 1875. [23] Curwen also copied *A Funeral Elegy* and sold the broadside at the same event.

Come rise up brother minute man and let us have a corous
The braver and the Bolder the more they will adore us
Oure contry cals for swords and Bals and Drums A loud Doth Rattle
Oure fifers charmes arise to arms Liberty cals to battle

We have from noble congras men elected for our nurses
And very joly farmer will assist us with their purses
We let them stay att home we say enjoy their with pleasure
And we will go and fight oure foes and save there Lives and treasure

So let us not be Dismayed alltho the tories thunder
Thay only want to Ruin us and live upon oure Plunder
Oure caus is just thirfore we must with heavens kind protection
With north and Gage in all thair rage will never cum in action

Now tew oure Station Let us march and randevuse with pleasure
We have ben like Brave minut men to sarve so Great A Treasure
We let them fit amediately that we are men of mettle
We Jarfey Boys that fere no nois will never flinch for Battle

Song of the Minute Man, courtesy
of the Harris Broadside Collection,
John Hay Library, Brown University

And when we Do return Again it will be with Glory
For them that Do remain at home to hear a valiant story
Thay will Draw nere and glad to hear no Douting of the wonder
That minut men though one to ten should bring tories under

And now poure Gage has tuck his flight and though he has left Commander
Lord North he has appointed to be his chief Defender
We fere them not though Bullits hot about oure heads Do rattle
Weal make them fit amediatley in such A Glorious Battle

Long may Georg live and rule the throne and all his loyal Subjects
That truly stands for liberty and makes these chief objections
For slavith chains we Do Disdain Likewise popesh tiriney
Such hellish frays we Do Defy and will not to yield to any

Cum fill us up abole Brave Boys it Better Dun than un Dun
Here is helth to thy Lord mayr and Livery of London
He in pure caus that made no paus Plead Boldly as they intended
For freedoms right with all oure might my Boys Let us Defend it

Let us be not Dismayd all though the tories should Defious
There is oure Brave melesi men that shurly will stand By us
That tory Brood that halth with stood that Grait and Glorious joyel
If theay Advance we will make them Dance the tune Yancadudal

TRADITIONAL – 1777

Song of the Minute Man.

1 Come rife up Brother minut men and let us have a corous
the braver and the Bolder the more they will adore us
oure contry cals for Swords and Bals and Drums A loud Doth rattle
oure fifers charmes arife to arms Liberty cals to batle

2 We have fum Noble congras men elected for our nurfes
And every joly farmer will affift us with thair purfes
we let them ftay att home we fay enjoy thaire wives with Pleafure
and we will go and fight oure foes and fave there Lives and treafure

3 So let us not be Dismayd alltho the tories thunder
Thay only want to Ruin us and live upon oure Plunder

Yankey Song

Yankey Song was composed by Mr. Bigelow of Salem and published in the *Salem Gazette* in July of 1811. This lively song was sung at a military celebration on the 4th of July at the Lynn Hotel in Lynn Massachusetts, and was also performed by the Federalists at Washington Hall in Salem "Its wit and pleasantry continues it a favorite with the Yankees." [24] *Yankee Doodle* will always be a favorite with Americans and "is so much superior to the vulgar ditties generally sung to this tune, that we think proper to preserve it. Some of the provincial phrases of New England are very happily ridiculed." [25]

Yankey Doodle is the tune, Americans delight in;
'Twill do to whistle, sing, or play, And just the thing for fighting.

  Chorus: Yankey Doodle, Boys; Huzza!
    Down outside-up the middle
    Yankey Doodle, fa, sol, la,
    Trumpet, Drum, and Fiddle.

Should Great Britain, Spain, or France, Wage war upon our shore, sir,
We'll lead them such a woundy dance, They'll find their toes are sore, sir.

Should a haughty foe we expect? To give our boys a caning,
We guess they'll find our boys have learned, A little bit of training.

I'll wager now a mug of flip, And bring it on the table,
Put Yankey boys aboard a ship, To beat them they are able.

Then if they go to argufy, I rather guess they'll find, too,
We've got a set of tonguey blades, T'out talk 'em, if they're mind to.

America's a dandy place; The people are all brothers;
And when one's got a pumpkin pie, He shares it with the others.

     Chorus: Yankey Doodle, Boys; Huzza!
           Down outside-up the middle
           Yankey Doodle, fa, sol, la,
           Trumpet, Drum, and Fiddle.

We work, and sleep, and pray, in peace— By industry we thrive, sir;
And if a drone won't do his part, We'll scout him from the hive, sir.

And then, on Independent Day, And who's a better right to?
We eat and drink, and sing and play, And have a dance at night, too.

Our girls are fair, our boys are tough, Our old folks wise and healthy;
And when we've every thing we want, We count that we are wealthy.

We're happy, free, and well to do, And cannot want for knowledge;
For, almost ev'ry mile or two, You find a school or college.

The land we till is all our own; Whate'er the price, we paid it;
Therefore we'll fight till all is blue, Should any dare invade it.

Since we're so bless'd, let's eat and drink With thankfulness and gladness:
Should we kick o'er our cup of joy, It would be satin madness.

     Chorus: Yankey Doodle, Boys; Huzza!
           Down outside-up the middle
           Yankey Doodle, fa, sol, la,
           Trumpet, Drum, and Fiddle.

MR.BIGELOW – 1806

Salem Quick Step

Salem Quick Step[26] was taken from *Howe's The Musician's Companion.*

TRADITIONAL – 1800s

Salem Cadet Band at Salem Willows Postcard, courtesy of Sal Pangallo

Salem Cadets' March

The *Salem Cadets' March*[27] was found in *Howe's School for the Clarinet* at the Boston Public Library and in the Library of Congress's sheet music collection.

TRADITIONAL – 1800s

Salem Cadets' March, Courtesy of the Boston Public Library

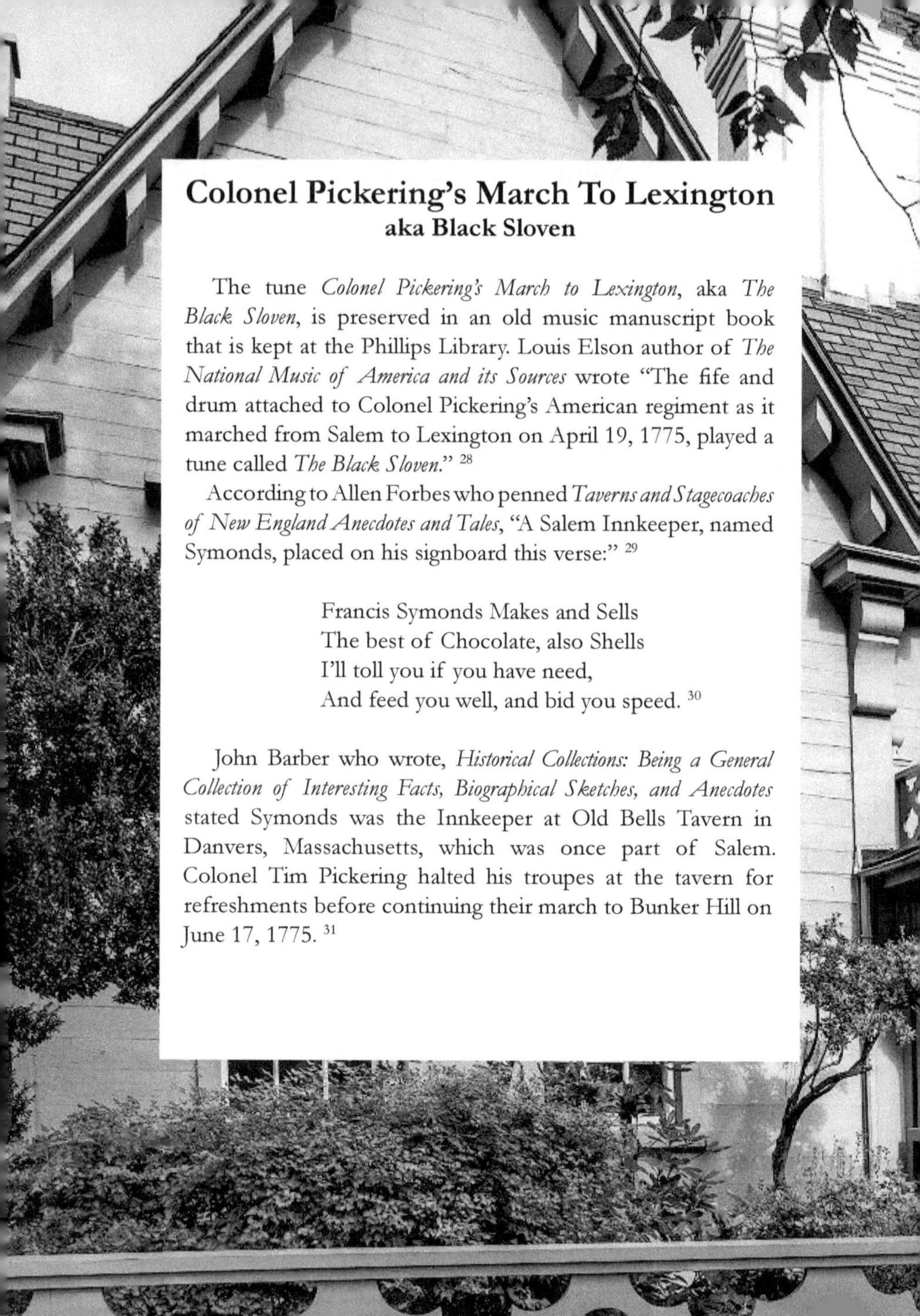

Colonel Pickering's March To Lexington
aka Black Sloven

The tune *Colonel Pickering's March to Lexington*, aka *The Black Sloven*, is preserved in an old music manuscript book that is kept at the Phillips Library. Louis Elson author of *The National Music of America and its Sources* wrote "The fife and drum attached to Colonel Pickering's American regiment as it marched from Salem to Lexington on April 19, 1775, played a tune called *The Black Sloven*." [28]

According to Allen Forbes who penned *Taverns and Stagecoaches of New England Anecdotes and Tales*, "A Salem Innkeeper, named Symonds, placed on his signboard this verse:" [29]

Francis Symonds Makes and Sells
The best of Chocolate, also Shells
I'll toll you if you have need,
And feed you well, and bid you speed. [30]

John Barber who wrote, *Historical Collections: Being a General Collection of Interesting Facts, Biographical Sketches, and Anecdotes* stated Symonds was the Innkeeper at Old Bells Tavern in Danvers, Massachusetts, which was once part of Salem. Colonel Tim Pickering halted his troupes at the tavern for refreshments before continuing their march to Bunker Hill on June 17, 1775. [31]

The Pickering House, courtesy of Mary Barker

Dreaming of Home and Mother

Dreaming of Home and Mother [32] was written in 1868 and composed by John P. Ordway. Ordway was born in Salem on August 1, 1824, and later moved to Boston as a young boy. Ordway wrote popular sentimental songs of the Civil War era. He graduated from Harvard Medical College in 1859 and was one of the first Union surgeons to volunteer at the beginning of the Civil War. He served in the Sixth Massachusetts Militia and was sent to tend the wounded after the Battle of Gettysburg. [33] While living in Boston, Ordway was on both the school board and in the Massachusetts House of Representatives. James Lord Peirpont, a friend of Ordway, wrote *The One Horse Open Sleigh*, later named *Jingle Bells*, and dedicated the song to John P. Ordway. [34] Peirpont also wrote the songs *No Nothing Polka* and *The Returned Californian*.

> Dreaming of home, dear old home.
> Home of childhood and mother-
> Oft when I wake 'tis sweet to find
> I've been dreaming of home and mother.
> Home, dear home, childhood's happy home!
> When I played with sister and with brother
> 'Twas the sweetest joy when we did roam
> Over hill and through dale with mother.

> Chorus: Dreaming of home, dear old home,
> Home of my childhood and mother-
> Oft When I wake 'tis sweet to find
> I've been dreaming of home and mother.

Sleep, balmy sleep, close mine eyes,
Keep me still thinking of mother-
Hark! It's her voice I seem to hear-
Yes, I'm dreaming of home und mother.
Angels come soothing me to rest,
I can feel their presence as none other,
For they sweetly say I shall be blest
With bright visions of home and mother.

Chorus: Dreaming of home, dear old home,
         Home of my childhood and mother-
         Oft When I wake 'tis sweet to find
         I've been dreaming of home and mother.

Childhood has come, come again.
Sleeping I see my dear mother-
See her loved form beside me kneel,
While I'm dreaming of home and mother.
Mother dear, whisper to me now,
Tell me of my sister and my brother-
Now I feel thy hand upon my brow-
Yes, I'm dreaming of home und mother.

Chorus: Dreaming of home, dear old home,
         Home of my childhood and mother-
         Oft When I wake 'tis sweet to find
         I've been dreaming of home and mother.

JOHN P. ORDWAY – 1851

Dreaming of Home and Mother,
courtesy of the Prints and Photographs
Division, Library of Congress

God Bless America
– A National Anthem –

This version of *God Bless America*[35] was composed and published as a patriotic song from World War I era by H. Leander D'Entremont of Salem in 1919.

OUR COUNTRY
God bless America,
The land of liberty
    From shore to shore:
May our flag glorious,
Ever victorious,
Be guardian over us
    For evermore, For evermore.

OUR PRESIDENT
God bless our President,
The faithful President
    Of this country,
That he be wisdom and light
To make the future bright
    For Liberty, For Liberty.

THE STARS AND STRIPES
God bless the stars and stripes;
The bright stars and broad stripes
    And field of blue:
Each star made history

Each stripe means victory,
That's what makes 'Old Glory'
          Faithful and true, Faithful and true.

OUR REPUBLIC
God bless our Republic,
The grandest Republic
          In all the world:
It's that posterity,
And all of humanity,
May reap prosperity,
          Our flag unfurled, Our flag unfurled.

OUR ARMY AND NAVY
To our noble Army
And our gallant NAVY,
          Thy blessings give:
Behind the guns they stand
To free the sea and land,
          That we may live, That we may live.

AN APPEAL TO GOD
O, Thou, Great God of Love,
Look from Thy Throne above,
          On us mortals:
We are Thy children still,
Grant us peace and goodwill,
And when we're thru life's grill
          Open Thy Portals, Open Thy Portals.

H. LEANDER D'ENTREMONT – 1919

God Bless America, courtesy of the World War I
Sheet Music Division, Library of Congress

SALEM ASSEMBLIES W

~ 6 ~

Commerce

TZES.

JEAN M. MISSUD.

Our Ride to Lynn

Our Ride to Lynn [1] was found in the broadside collection at the Phillips Library. The ballad is about several young men on an adventurous ride to Lynn and their trip back to Salem. As they enter Salem, they pass the tollhouse, pay their toll, and head home. *Our Ride to Lynn* is sung to the tune of *Willie on the Dark Blue Sea* written by Boston composer, H. S. Thompson.

> This day we've got a horse and chaise,
> To ride far over to Lynn
> And many a pleasant hour will pass,
> Ere we come home again.

> Chorus: We're bound to have a first rate time,
>   Of pleasure drink our fill;
>   And as the day is very fine,
>   Enjoy ourselves we will.

> The sun is shining bright and clear,
> The breeze is blowing free,
> The trees in autumn's hues are drest,
> The birds sing merrily.

> Here, on the crest of this high hill,
> We view the ocean blue;
> Now through the valley swift we speed,
> With our merry, happy crew!

Old Turnpike (now Highland Ave) Guarded by Toll Gate, *Salem Evening News*, Tuesday January 23, 1923

> Ah! Here we are, in sight of Lynn!
> Now, through its streets we ride:
> And as we swiftly go, we see
> New scenes on every side.

In every street, in every lane,
Some pretty lass we meet;
But when compared with Salem bells,
They are not half so sweet.

The sun is sleeping in the west,
The night comes on apace:
We'll leave Lynn city far behind,
Home, through the woods we'll race.

The moon is sailing through the sky,
The twinkling stars appear;
And over the road, the tall trees cast
Their shadows far and near.

      Chorus: We're bound to have a first rate time
                  Of pleasure drink our fill;
                  And as the night is very fine,
                  Enjoy ourselves we will.

We pass the toll-house swiftly by,
Scarce stop to pay our scot;
And now we enter Essex Street
Upon a handsome trot.

The Old Toll House, *Salem Evening News*, Tuesday January 23, 1923

      Chorus: Yes, we a pleasant time have had,
                  Seen many a thing that's new,
                  Seen many a joyous, sprightly, lad,
                  And many a lassie too.

J.C. DUCHOW – 1850

The First Trip

The First Trip was written by Edwin Jocelyn. According to Francis C. Bradlee in an article in the *Essex Institute Collection*, the ballad is about the launching of the Salem and Lowell Railroad as it was described in the *Salem Gazette* on August 2, 1850. The Salem Glee Club sang the ballad at the opening ceremony of the railroad. [2]

Twas seven o'clock on Thursday morn,
And things were ready all,
We step'd on board the Railway cars,
On neighbors just to call;
The steam was up — the iron horse
Was proud to bear his load;
Away we shot, on this first trip,
Upon the Lowell Road!

Chorus: O, the Railroad! You're the way for me!
      No other mode is half so sweet. So jolly, fleet and free!

We flew across old Danvers town,
And made the people stare;
And then we pounced on Middleton,
And found a welcome there;
And, next, we call'd on Reading folks,
But only left our card;
That we should make so short a stop
They thought it vey-hard.

Chorus: O, the Railroad! You're the way for me!
      No other mode is half so sweet. So jolly, fleet and free!

At Tewksb'ry, next, we found ourselves,
And found the people glad,

For who, the jolly, flying cars
Could view with feelings sad?
Away to Lowell's busy spot
The speeding train now whirls,
And soon we hail the blessed sight
Of Fact'ries, Men and Girls!

Chorus: O, the Railroad! You're the way for me!
      No other mode is half so sweet. So jolly, fleet and free!

Now, here's a note to Phillips' name!
A noble work he's done,
The int'rests of two cities fair
Has mingled into one!
He's built a wharf for Lowell's trade,
Old ocean's wealth to bear,
To ancient Salem's western bound
Annex'd a city fair!

Chorus: O, the Railroad! You're the way for me!
      No other mode is half so sweet. So jolly, fleet and free!

Hurrah! the track is ready now!
And we will have you know
The transport, to and fro, shall be
A caution to the slow!
Upon our borders, fresh and fair
The Merrimac shall glide;
And to its favorite city's view
The ocean open wide.

Chorus: O, the Railroad! You're the way for me!
      No other mode is half so sweet. So jolly, fleet and free!

EDWIN JOCELYN, ESQ. – 1850

Hardware Advertisement

This advertisement is from a hardware store that was located on Essex Street in Salem and published in the *Salem Gazette* on July 11, 1800. The announcement was meant; "To be Said or Sung" [3] but no tune was ever written.

Cross-cut saws and handsaw files,
  As many as you please, Sirs.
Hammers to, all very new,
  And buttons for your sleeves, Sirs.

Razors and scissors of good stuff,
  With Cabinets and knives, Sirs.
Bottles neat, that smells quite sweet,
  Suitable for your wife, Sirs.

Britannia ware, that will with ease,
  Stand by you all your life, Sirs.
Toasting rack, and fins in packs,
  With Glasses for your eyes, Sirs.

Watch chains rare, some made of half,
  With seals and keys of brass, Sirs.
Afforded all, both great and small,
  That they made better pass, Sirs.

Lock keys, buckle for knees,
  With pocket books and purses.
Half pint sacks, and castin 'd tacks,
  And good elastic Truffles.

TRADITIONAL – 1800

Irish Economy

The humorous ditty *Irish Economy*[4] was found in the *Salem Gazette*
dated February 18, 1820.

While Pat and Tom, with various talks.
Pass'd off the time one morning walk.
The conversation changed to rove,
Upon a new invented stove.

Says Tom," I think this new invention
Deserves each prudent man's attention;
This stove will answer (as they say)
----------------place every way-

For every purpose this as good
and one will save full half your wood."
"Eye, Eye." says Pat, why what a notion,
You Yankees are for calculations-

If what you tell is true, my jewel-
When what needless thing is fuel.
No more I'll use it, no not I,
Bet straight a pair of stoves I'll buy,

See one save half-now, by my soul.
I'll get me two and save the whole.

TRADITIONAL – 1820

Apprenticed In Salem

Apprenticed in Salem [5] recorded on Peter Johnson's CD, *Newport's Fair Town; Traditional Songs and Ballads of North America*. The *Apprenticed in Salem* is a variation of *Blow the Candle Out* or *The London Apprentice*. Peter states in his liners notes, "this song is not as bawdy as some of its British cousins, but is refreshingly frank in the easy acceptance of the pleasurable aspects of love without doom and gloom of sin and salvation found in many of the southern mountain ballads." [5] Early versions of these ballads can be found in the Bodleian's digital collections of ballads. [6] The town of "Salem" could be substituted with almost any town's name.

When I was an apprentice in Salem,
I went to see my dear.
The candles were all burning,
The moon so bright and clear.
I knocked upon her window,
To ease her of her pain.
She rose to let me in,
and she barred the door again.

I like your well'd behavior'
and thus I often say,
I cannot rest contented,
With you so far away.
The roads they are so muddy,
You can gain about,
Come roll me in your arms love,
and blow the candles out.

Your father and your mother,
In yonder room do lie,
A-huggin one another,
So why not you and I?
A-huggin one another,
Without fear or doubt,
Come roll me in your arms my love,
and blow the candle out.

If I prove successful love,
We'll name it after me,
Keep it neat and kiss it,
and tap it on your knee.
When 3 years are over,
My time it will be out,
and I will double my ineptness,
By blowing the candle out.

TRADITIONAL – 1813

William R. Warner,
The New England Blacking Man

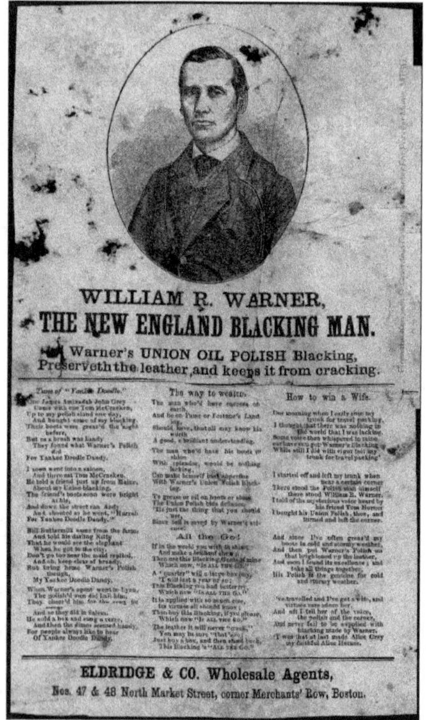

The New England Blacking Man was found in the Broadside Collection at the Center for Popular Music at Middle Tennessee State University. Warner's Union Oil Polish Company sent salesmen throughout the towns of Lynn and Salem singing the song to the tune of *Yankee Doodle Dandy* while hawking blacking boot polish that "preserves the leather and keeps it from cracking" [7]

The New England Blacking Man, courtesy of the Kenneth S. Goldstein Collection of American Song Broadsides Center for Popular Music, Middle Tennessee State University

The New England Blacking Man

One James Aminadab John Grey,
Come with one Tom McCracken.
Up to his polish stand one day,
And bought some of my blacking.

Their boots were greas'd the night before,
But as a brush was handy.
They found what Warner's Polish did,
For Yankee Doodle Dandy.

I went into a saloon,
And there sat Tom McCracken.
He told his friends just up from Maine,
About my Union blacking.
The friend's boots soon were bright as his,
And down the street ran Andy.
And shouted as he went, "Hurrah,
For Yankee Doodle Dandy."

Bill Buttermilk came from the farm,
And told his darling Kitty.
That he would see the elephant,
When he got to the city.
Don't go too near the maid replied,
And, oh, keep clear of brandy.
But bring home Warner's Polish though,
My Yankee Doodle Dandy.

When Warner's agent went to Lynn,
The polish'd men did hail him.
They cheer'd him for the song he sang,
And so they did in Salem.
He sold a box and sung a verse,
And then the dimes seemed handy.
For people always like to hear,
Of Yankee Doodle Dandy.

TRADITIONAL - 1850

Salem Willows Fo

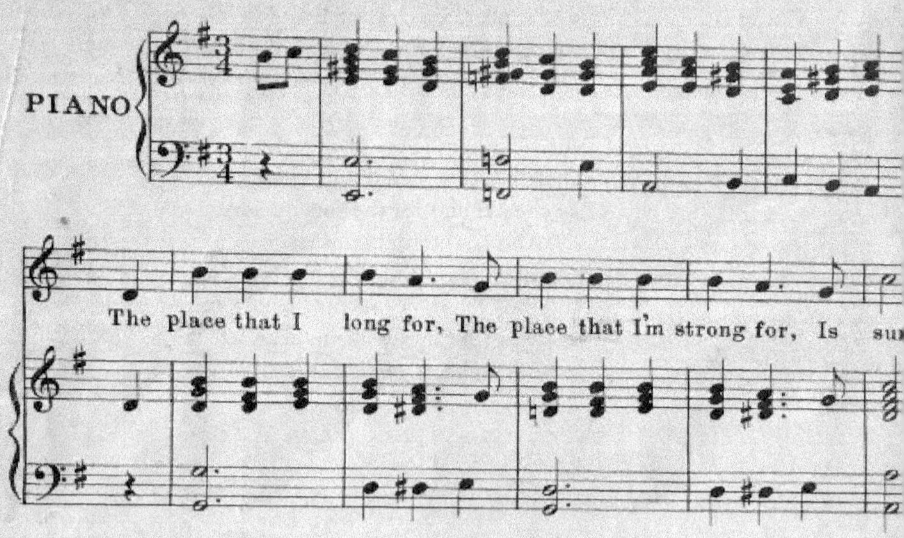

~ 7 ~

Dancing

ine
By LOU COLLINS
and GEO. HARDY
Arr. by BERT BURHOE
be in the race, The

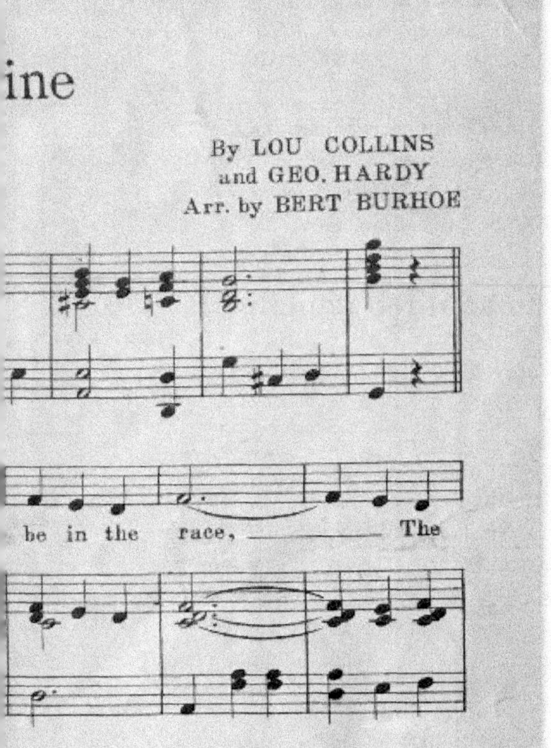

Dancing

Salem has a long history of social dancing and traditional music. The early colonists brought a love for dancing with them that not even the hardships of the country could suppress. [1]

The first evidence of a public dance in Salem comes from the diary of Benjamin Lynde, Jr. His entry on July 14, 1730 reads: Raining while at Survey's dance. There are many couples. I did not dance and stayed till 7 o'clock. [2] Since ballrooms were nonexistent, dancing was done in homes. Milton Hehr writes in his dissertation, *Musical Activities in Salem, Massachusetts*, "It was recorded in Mrs. Holyoke's Diary that she attended at least one dance (in various homes) a year between the years of 1761 and 1781 with the exception of the years 1762, 66, 70, 75, 76, and 80." [3] Below are four of Mrs. Holyoke's diary entries:

> January 15, 1761 a dance Jefferies' in the evening.
> January 29, 1761 a dance Jefferies'.
> February 26, 1761 at a dance at Jefferies.
> November 24, 1762 dance, not there, snow. [4]

To a **LADY** who admired dancing

To a LADY who admired dancing [5] was found in the *Salem Mercury*, a local newspaper dated July 29, 1788.

> MAY I presume in humble lays,
> My dancing fair, thy steps to praise?
> While this grand maxim I advance,
> That all the world is but a dance,

That human-kind, both man and woman,
Do dance is evident and common.
David himself, that God-like king,
We know could dance, as well as sing.

Folks who at court would keep their ground,
Must dance the year attendance round.
All nature is one ball, we find:
The water dances to the wind;

The sea itself at night and noon
Rises and capers to the moon;
The moon around the earth does tread
A Cheshire round in buxom red;

The earth and planets round the sun
Dance, nor will their dance be done
'Till nature in one mass is blended;
Then we may say the ball is ended.

TRADITIONAL – 1788

The Assembly Hall at the corner of present day Chestnut Street and Cambridge Street in Salem opened in 1769. The hall was used for lectures, fencing, violin lessons, dance classes, singing concerts, juggling, and feats of strengths, as well as other activities. [6] Two of the most memorable functions held there during its relatively brief history took place in the spring of 1774. On April 28th Salem's Tories gathered at the hall to bid farewell to Governor Thomas Hutchinson who was leaving for England. Five weeks later many of the same citizens returned to welcome Hutchinson's replacement, Thomas Gage. [7] On the evening of June 6th a brilliant ball was held at the Assembly Room in honor of Thomas Gage. [8]

The Assembly Hall was replaced as the gathering spot for the town's wealthier citizens with a new function hall that was built on Federal Street in 1872 and was funded by Salem's merchant class. George Washington was honored with a ball in the hall during his visit to Salem on October 28, 1789. Five years earlier, the Assembly House was the scene of a similar party for the Marquis de Lafayette. [9]

Assembly House Postcard,
courtesy of Sal Pangallo

The Assembly House,
courtesy of Mary Barker

The Flirtation

The Flirtation [10] was found in the *Salem Gazette*, May 30, 1788.

YE dear pretty ladies,
Who now in your gay days,
So merrily take your diversion,

116

Sure there is no sporting
Compar'd unto courting,
And having a little flirtation.
And having a little flirtation.

What tho' now you call,
An assembly or ball,
A pleasant and sweet recreation;
How soon would you treat it,
As dull and insipid,
Had you not a little flirtation.
Had you not a little flirtation.

In church or in street,
Or wherever you meet,
The object of your inclination;
Oh! Is it not pleasure,
Beyond any measure,
To have a dear little flirtation.
To have a dear little flirtation.

There's you, and there's you,
And there's you, madam too,
And there's you, in your sly situation,
Tho' you all look so shy,
Yet you cannot deny,
That you're fond of a little flirtation.
That you're fond of a little flirtation.

TRADITIONAL – 1788

Newhall's March

In 1788, Benjamin Gardner of Marblehead and in 1805, Joshua Cushing of Salem notated songbooks that documented fife and drum music. Most of these tunes were also performed for dances. Many of the pieces including: *Fisher's Hornpipe*, *Soldier's Joy*, *Boston March*, *Yankee Doodle*, *New Rigged Ship*, and *Jefferson and Liberty* were played into the next century and are also performed today. Some melodies have a direct Salem connection like *Salem Artillery*, *Lailson's Ride*, and *Newhall's March*. [11] Fred Finkle, a fiddle player from Marblehead, found and shared *Newhall's March* with the Salem Country Orchestra circa 2008, but no one is sure where he got the tune.

TRADITIONAL – UNKNOWN

118

Lailson's Ride

T. William (Bill) Smith, a local contra dance musician discovered *Lailson's Ride* [12] in the manuscript collection at the Phillips Library. Smith transcribed the tune circa 1980 and played it with the Salem Country Orchestra over the next 25 years. The tune's formal connection to Salem is unknown. However, it was transcribed by a musician in the early 1800s and then stored in the Phillips Library.

The Maid With Elbows Bare

The Maid With Elbows Bare [13] was found in the *Salem Gazette*, #1223, May 17, 1803.

Let Tasteless lover chant their lays,
To please the modest, full dress fair;
The talk remains for me, to praise
The charming maid with elbows bare.

Her ruddy cheek, her sparking eyes,
Her coral lips, her -------- hair,
All are the charms I highly prize,
But not so much as elbows bare!

The unveiled bosom-neck of snow-
May tempt the ill-bred clown of stares,
But first-rate beaux with deference bow,
Before the maid with elbows bare.

Some ladies show the ankle's shape,
A fashion too not very rare;
Others expose a pretty nape,
Not mine's the maid with elbows bare.

Let her, in that loose flowing robe
Which flaunts and flutters in the air,
Reflects a heart the ne'er will probe,
Unless she leaves her elbows bare.

When winter storms are near and cold,
And keenly blows the northern air,
When muffs and furs the limbs unfold,
Still trips my maid with elbows bare.

When summer's scorching heat prevails,
And veils shut out the sun's bright glares,
Still, still my maid will never fail
To go with graceful elbows bare.

In winter, summer, fall or spring,
In weather either foul or fair,
In days or night, the charms I sing,
Of my sweat maid with elbows bare.

TRADITIONAL – 1803

Chestnut Street

HENRY. K. OLIVER – 1848

Hamilton Hall on Chestnut Street in Salem hosted elaborate celebrations honoring various local and visiting dignitaries, as well as social dances. [14] Famous architect and master woodcarver, Samuel McIntire of Salem, designed Hamilton Hall in 1805. The Hall is considered one of the most important Federal style buildings in America and is designated as a National Historic Landmark. It has been a vibrant part of the community for over two hundred years. The tune *Chestnut Street* was written by Henry K. Oliver of Salem and is still sung today at Sacred Harp sings, traditional sacred choral music that originated in New England. [15]

Chestnut Street, courtesy of the Boston Public Library

A New Song

Marianne C. D. Silsbee of Salem published a book called *A Half Century in Salem* in 1887. The book consisted of stories that she read at house parties and other events in Salem. Silsbee stated that she wrote the book "for the amusement of friends who may not be adverse to refreshing their memories with harmless gossip." [16]

Hamilton Hall, courtesy of Sal Pangallo

Hamilton Hall, courtesy of Mary Barker

One of Silsbee's stories was titled *Hamilton Hall.* The author stated the Salem Assemblies (social dances) were revived at Hamilton Hall in 1859 after a two-year hiatus. [17] A Lady's Ball was given to celebrate the end of the season. Mr. Remond, a caterer who had worked at Hamilton Hall since 1805, sent a large bowl to be used at the function. [18] Silsbee gives credit to an elderly woman for writing *A New Song* about the famed bowl.

A New Song

When this old bowl was new
The magnates of the land.
In numbers not a few,
Did form a joyous band;
And many a stately dame,
So beautiful to view,
To our assemblies came,
When this old bowl was new.

Then ladies bright did shine
In loveliness and pride;
While draped in muslin fine
The maidens fair did glide
Then waved the ostrich plume
O'er matrons grand and true
In our assembly room,
When this old bowl was new.

Knee buckles then appeared
With silken hose they say;
The rules of Fashion feared,
All bore despotic sway,
Then gentlemen were dressed
In coat of broadcloth blue,
With white and spotless vest,
When this old bowl was new.

The courtly minuet
And long lined country dance
(For beaux and belles as yet
Had no quadrilles from France)

Were seen upon the floor,
As the dancers swam or flew,
With graces hovering o'er,
When this old bowl was new.

When supper time came then,
The Elder Ladies proud
Were led by gallant men
Out through the waiting crowd,
The younger came in place,
Their place full well they knew,
And yielded with a grace,
When this old bowl was new.

The good old times are fled,
Have vanished far away;
The stately dames are dead,
The men oh where are they?
The minuet is a dream,
Or like a tale that is told;
The light doth faintly beam,
Now that new bowl is old.

Yet Salem numbers still
Her daughter's fresh and fair,
Who dance with right good will,
And silks and laces wear,
Their watch spring hoops are wide,
Gowns hang in plenteous fold,
And they are Salem's pride,
Now that new bowl is old.

Bright eyes are glancing yet,
Fair checks are blushing on;

But where Old Ladies sat
I gaze they all are gone.
No Elders now are sung,
The deed would be too bold;
America is young
Now that new bowl is old.

The gallants of today,
In solemn suits of black,
Still make the ballroom gay,
While outward show they lack.
Yes we can praise them too,
Nor leave their worth untold,
Though old times now are new,
And that new bowl is old.

BY AN ELDERLY LADY – 1887

After the dance ended, the bowl was returned to Mr. Remond. Silsbee wrote that Mr. Remond sent a letter to the *Salem Gazette* describing Hamilton Hall and the bowl's history.[18] Sometime during the two years the Salem Assemblies were not held at Hamilton Hall, the bowl went missing. Mr. Remond found the bowl at "Higginson Square" and returned it to Hamilton Hall. Silsbee transcribed the conclusion of the letter by Mr. Remond describing the bowl, "The writer has no ambition to gratify, and nothing for which to ask, but to preserve the Old Bowl. Cherish the hall; let it stand and keep it untarnished for its intended purpose." [19]

Social Dancing continued at Hamilton Hall throughout the 1900s and to the present day. One of Hamilton Hall's oldest traditions is the annual Christmas Dance. The dance is held each December as a fundraiser and dates back to the 1880s.

Pop! Goes the Weasel

This version of *Pop! Goes the Weasel* comes from Fred A. Gannon's *Old Salem Scrap Book II*. [20] Gannon noted that young girls in Salem during the 1890s would sing the melody of *Pop! Goes the Weasel* and make up lines to fit the music. Gannon goes on to write, "When Grandmother was a girl and went to dances at Hamilton Hall or a party, she joined in the singing of songs like this." [20] The Authors James and Dorothy Volo wrote in their book, *Family Life in Seventeenth and Eighteenth Century America*, that the skeining process, the winding of yard to form a skein of uniform thickness, inspired many versions of *Pop! Goes the Weasel*. [21]

Queen Victoria's very sick,
Napoleon's got the measles
Sebastopol is won at last.
Pop! Goes the weasel.

All around the cobbler's house
The monkey chased the people
And after them in double haste
Pop! Went the Weasel.

When the night walks in as black as sheep
And the hen and her eggs are fast asleep
When in to her nest a serpent creeps,
Pop! Goes the Weasel.

Of all the dance that ever was plann'd
To galvanize the heel and hand
There's none (that moved) so gay (and grand)
Pop! Goes the Weasel.

TRADITIONAL – 1890

Dancing Instruction

M. C. D. Silsbee describes various types of social dances in her book *A Half Century in Salem*. She wrote that "a voluntary" is a dance for which the gentlemen were at "liberty to engage their partners." A draw-dance is a lottery, which the ladies and gentlemen pick numbers, and dance with the corresponding number. Silsbee stated that they "might or might not be especially pleased with their luck." [23]

DANCING

MR. STIMSON

RESPECTFULLY informs the inhabitants of Salem that his School, for the instruction of Masters and Misses in the polite accomplishment of DANCING, will commence on Tuesday, April 18th, 5 o'clock P. M. at Hamilton (upper) Hall, Chesnut Street.

Dancing Academy

MR. PARKS,

INSTRUCTER OF DANCING,

MOST respectfully informs the Ladies and Gentlemen of Salem and its vicinity, that he intends opening a School for the instruction of Masters and Misses in the pleasing and graceful accomplishment of DANCING, at Franklin Hall, on Monday the 10th day of April next

The most respectable references can be given. For further particulars please apply at this office, or at the Essex Coffee House.

Salem, March 21. 1820.

Dancing and Dancing Academy,
Salem Gazette March 21, 1820

Dancing School—opened.

MR. BOSSIEUX has the honour to inform the public that he has opened his Dancing School in Franklin Hall, *Tuesdays* and *Fridays*—for Ladies, from 3 to 6, and for Gentlemen, from 6 to 9 o'clock, P. M. And every Friday he will teach Cotillion figures, with new

Music & Dancing Academy.

FRANCIS MAURICE presents his Compliments to the Ladies and Gentlemen of Salem and Marblehead, and returns them his unfeigned thanks for the liberal encouragement he has experienced for a number of months past. Should it be continued, Mr. Maurice assures the Ladies and Gentlemen, who may entrust their Children to his care, that his best endeavours shall not be wanting, to improve their manners, and in perfecting them in the elegant accomplishment of Dancing.

SPRING SCHOOL.

The School will be kept twice in a week. In the afternoon from 3 o'clock until sun set, for the small Class—and from sun set until 10 in the evening, for the larger Class. TERMS—8 dollars per Quarter, half to be paid at entrance, and the remainder at the end of the Quarter. Should 25 subscribers appear, the School will begin on the 1st of April next. Subscriptions will be received by Mr Maurice at his Lodgings, at Mrs. Baldwin's.

Dancing School, *Salem Gazette*, January 25, 1820 Vol. XXXIV Number 7, Music and Dancing Academy, *Impartial Register*, March 12 1801 Vol. II No. 88

Dancing instruction was held throughout Salem in the 1800s to learn the various styles of dance. Francis Maurice, dancing instructor, placed advertisements in the *Impartial Register*, a local Salem newspaper for classes being held at his Music and Dancing Academy in 1801. Mr. Stimson held dance classes in the upper hall of Hamilton Hall while Mr. Bossieux and Mr. Parks held instruction at their dance schools in Franklin Hall, sight of the Hawthorne Hotel, in the 1820s. Instruction was also given at Walsh's Dancing Academy located at 4 Lafayette Street in 1880. Henry O. Upton used the Cadet Hall for his dancing school classes, and performances in the 1890s. [24]

Pyncheon Lane Capric

Henry O. Upton wrote *Pyncheon Lane Capric* in 1892. The dance tune is one in a series of tunes written for the *House of Seven Gables Series*. The other tunes written for the series are called *The Caper* (A Dance with Full Explanation) and *Galop, "The Crickets."* Upton was born in 1839 in Salem and was a member of the Salem Brass Band and one of the original members of the Salem Cadet Band. He began studying and teaching social dancing in Salem in 1864. [25]

Pyncheon Lane Capric, part of the *House of the Seven Gables Series*, courtesy of the House of the Seven Gables Settlement Association

HENRY O. UPTON – 1892

The Upton family purchased the House of the Seven Gables in 1883 and lived there for the next 25 years. They welcomed visitors to view the house and promoted its connection to Nathaniel Hawthorne. The house was sold to Caroline Emmerton in 1908 and the Uptons moved to Salem Neck. Henry lived there until his death in 1919. [26]

Salem Willows for Mine

As social dancing continued in downtown Salem, much larger dance halls were beginning to be built in an area of Salem called the Willows overlooking the Atlantic Ocean and Beverly harbor. John McDonald a Salem Willow's resident was quoted in The *Salem Evening News* saying, "The best bands in the country used to come to the Salem Willows." They played in the ballroom casinos and entertained hundreds of people from Salem and the surrounding area. [27] Lou Collins and trumpeter, George Hardy composed *Salem Willows For Mine*. The song was published in 1919 by L. A. Collins and dedicated to Mr. W. E. Brown. [28] Brown was the lessee and manager of the Casino Ballroom in the Salem Willows.

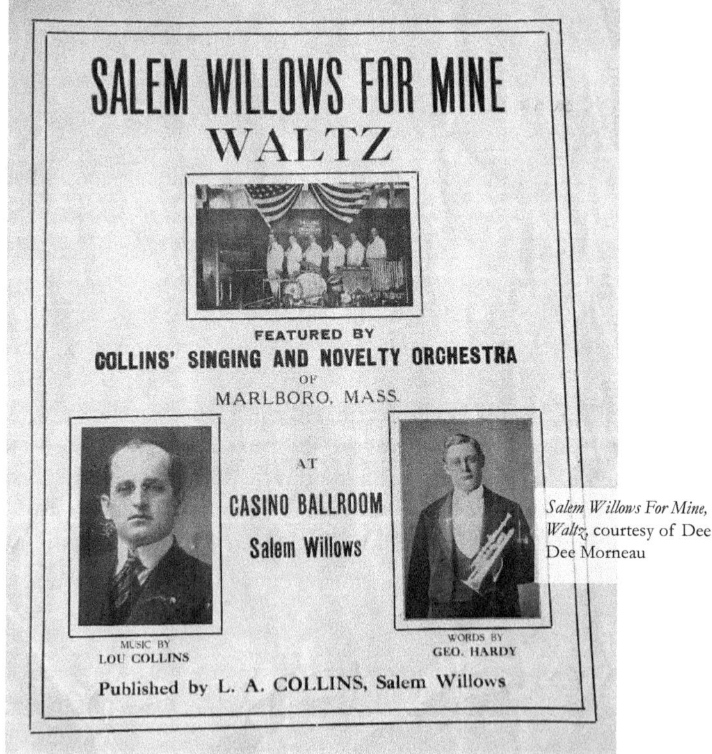

Salem Willows For Mine, Waltz, courtesy of Dee Dee Morneau

The Salem Willows For Mine

The place that I long for, the place that I'm strong for,
Is sure to be in the race,
The boys who will meet you, The girls who will greet you,
Will all have a smile on their face,

It's not very far from Salem, and from Lynn it's a half hour's ride.
You don't mind the trolley,
Because you can jolly,
The nice little girls by your side.

On moonlights, Gee! it is dandy, and on Sundays its simply divine.
You can have all your "Coney's"
To me they're all phoneys
But Salem Willows for mine.

The dear ballroom floor, is the place I adore,
The waters with nice shady views,
The music is grand, Makes you dance, understand,
It's the place where you'll never feel blue.

It's not very far from Salem, and from Lynn it's a half hour's ride.
You don't mind the trolley,
Because you can jolly,
The nice little girls by your side.

On moonlights, Gee! it is dandy, and on Sundays its simply divine.
You can have all your "Coney's"
To me they're all phoneys
But Salem Willows for mine.

LOU COLLINS AND GEORGE HARDY – 1919

Salem Country Dance

Salem residents T. William (Bill) and Sarah Smith continued the tradition of offering monthly dances in Salem between 1980 and 2008 at both the Grace Church and the Tabernacle Church. The Smith's love for traditional dance music and for a dance community kept them active and involved in Salem until they moved to Belfast, Maine in 2009. Chris Greene a Salem resident and dance enthusiast designed the Salem Country Dance flyer circa 1982. [29]

Salem Country Dance flyer, from Author's Personal Collection

Social dancing continues to this day in Salem. The Commonwealth Vintage Dancers celebrated their eleventh annual dance in December 2019. The Fezziwig's Ball is held annually at Old Town Hall in downtown Salem. The ball highlights the Christmas season during the mid 1800s with vintage dress and dancing. The program consists of Victorian favorites as *Pop Goes the Weasel*, the *Virginia Reel*, contra dances, simple quadrilles, polkas, and a waltz. [30]

Salem's newest Hamilton Hall dance event "The Resistance Ball," celebrates the Colonists peaceful confrontation with British Colonel Alexander Leslie and his troops in 1775. [31]

High Street

T. William (Bill) Smith wrote *High Street* in 2012. Bill led the Salem Country Orchestra for over twenty-five years. High Street is where Bill and his wife Sarah lived while living in Salem. *High Street* was recorded on Bill's CD entitled *Strawberry Jam*. [32]

Spring Son[g]

FOR

FOUR FEMALE VOICES

WITH

Pianoforte Accompaniment

BY

G. W. Chadwic[k]

Op. 9.

~ 8 ~
Courtship

When I Saw Sweet Nellie Home

Both *When I Saw Sweet Nellie Home* and *Seeing Nellie Home* have a connection to Salem, but there is some confusion over who wrote the songs. *Seeing Nellie Home* was an American song first published in the 1850s under the title *When I Saw Sweet Nellie Home*. It was composed and arranged by John Fletcher and Frances Kyle. In subsequent versions of the song some of the lyrics were changed. The tune has also been referred to as *Aunt Dinah's Quilting Party*. [1] Robert B. Waltz from Fresno State University stated:

> The early history of this song is slightly confused. It first appeared in 1856, but evidently in an unauthorized edition perhaps taken from a minstrel troupe performance. In 1859, the composer, John Fletcher, issued an official edition complete with complaints about the previous editions.[2]

When I Saw Sweet Nellie Home

In the sky the bright stars glittered, on the grass the moonlight fell,
Unshed the sound of daylight's bustle, closed the pink-eyed pimpernel;
As down the moss-grown wood path, where the cattle love to roam.
From Aunt Dinah's quilting party I was seeing Nelly home.

Chorus: When I saw sweet Nelly home,
        When I saw sweet Nelly home;
        How I bless the August evening,
        When I saw sweet Nelly home.

Jetty ringlets softly flattered o'er her brow as white as snow.
And her cheek, the crimson sunset, scarcely had a warmer glow;
'Mid her parted lips' Vermillion, white teeth flashed like ocean foam;
All I marked with pulses throbbing, as I saw sweet Nelly home.

Chorus: When I saw sweet Nelly home,
         When I saw sweet Nelly home;
         How I bless the August evening,
         When I saw sweet Nelly home.

When the autumn tinged the greenwood, turning all the leaves to gold,
In the lawn by alders shaded, I my love to Nelly told;
As we stood together, gazing on the star-bespangled dome,
How I blessed the August evening when I saw sweet Nelly home.

Chorus: When I saw sweet Nelly home,
         When I saw sweet Nelly home;
         How I bless the August evening,
         When I saw sweet Nelly home.

White hairs mingle with my tresses; furrows steal upon my brow,
Nor a love-smile cheers and blesses life's declining moments now.
Matron in a snowy 'kerchief, closer to my bosom come.
Tell me, dost thou still remember when I saw sweet Nellie home?

Chorus: When I saw sweet Nelly home,
         When I saw sweet Nelly home;
         How I bless the August evening,
         When I saw sweet Nelly home.

FRANCES KYLE & JOHN FLETCHER – 1856/59

Nicholas E. Tawa author of the book, *Arthur Foote: A Musician in the Frame of Time and Place*, writes Arthur Foote was an American classical composer born in Salem in 1853, [3] who may have played either one of these two popular ballads. Tawa further states that Foote wrote an accompaniment to the melody, which was published in the 1874 Harvard songbook; however, the book has not been located. [4]

Seeing Nellie Home

In the sky the bright stars glittered
On the bank the pale moon shone
It was from Aunt Dinah's quilting party
I was seeing Nellie home.

> Chorus: I was seeing Nellie home,
> I was seeing Nellie home.
> It was from Aunt Dinah's quilting party,
> I was seeing Nellie home

On my arm a soft hand rested
Rested light as ocean foam
It was from Aunt Dinah's quilting party
I was seeing Nellie home.

> Chorus: I was seeing Nellie home,
> I was seeing Nellie home.
> It was from Aunt Dinah's quilting party,
> I was seeing Nellie home

On my lips a whisper trembled
Trembled till it dared to come
It was from Aunt Dinah's quilting party
I was seeing Nellie home.

> Chorus: I was seeing Nellie home,
> I was seeing Nellie home.
> It was from Aunt Dinah's quilting party,
> I was seeing Nellie home.

On my life new hopes were dawning
And those hopes have lived and grown
It was from Aunt Dinah's quilting party
I was seeing Nellie home.

Chorus: I was seeing Nellie home,
I was seeing Nellie home.
It was from Aunt Dinah's quilting party,
I was seeing Nellie home.

PATRICK S. GILMORE – 1856

Fred Gannon, author of the *Old Salem Scrap Book*, said, "P. S. Gilmore wrote the song *Seeing N'ellie Home*, of a maid in Salem." [5] According to the writers of the television program *The Walton's*, *Seeing Nellie Home* was written by Louis Lambert (aka P. S. Gilmore) for the show's Quilting episode. [6]

Johnny Cash also sang a version of *Seeing Nellie Home*, which has made this song's connection to Salem even more interesting. Cash learned through a genealogist that he was of Scottish descent: In the early 1600s, a mariner named William Cash sailed from Scotland to Salem carrying a cargo of pilgrim voyagers. [7]

Additionally, Rosanne Cash, Johnny Cash's daughter, wrote in a *New York Times* article titled *Measure for Measure; Time Travel and the Ballad Tradition* dated February 7, 2014 that she had told her son that he had Cash ancestors on both sides of the Civil War. [8] While tracing their lineage in the Civil War database, Rosanne discovered the photograph of a William Cash who was a lieutenant in the Massachusetts Eighth Infantry and also a photograph of a William Cash that served in several Southern regiments. This all makes sense because historical records show the arrival of the first Cash in Salem, Massachusetts, during the 17th century. [8]

Twinkling Stars Are Laughing, Love

Twinkling Stars Are Laughing, Love [9] was found in the Lester S. Levy Collection of Sheet Music. The song was published in 1855 and composed by Salem native John P. Ordway, later the leader of the Boston based Ordway's Aeolians.

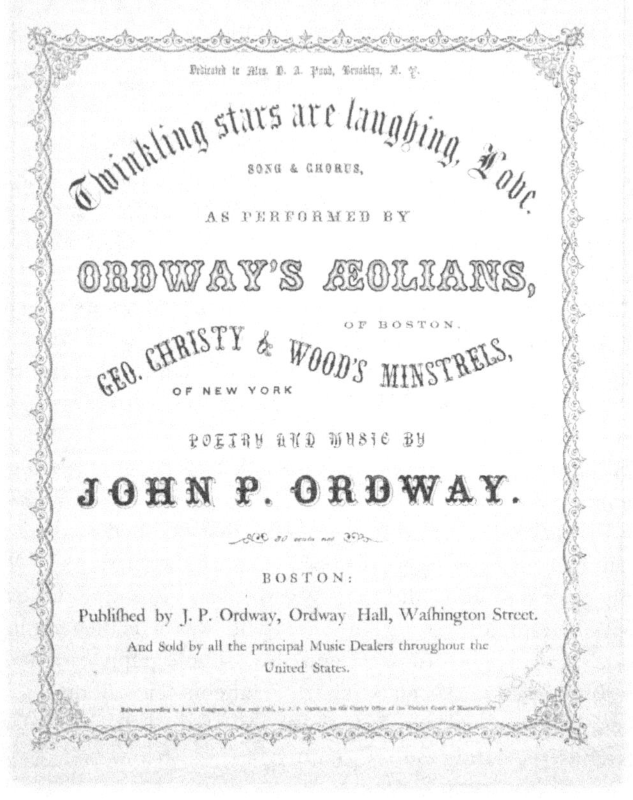

Twinkling Stars Are Laughing, Love, courtesy of Lester S. Levy Collection of Sheet Music, Sheridan Libraries, Johns Hopkins University

Twinkling Stars Are Laughing Love

Twinkling stars are laughing love,
Laughing on you and me;
While your bright eyes look in mine,
Peeping stars they seem to be.
Troubles come and go, love,
Brightest scenes must leave our sight;
But the star of hope, love,
Shines with radiant beams tonight.

    Chorus: Twinkling stars are laughing love,
           Laughing on you and me;
           While your bright eyes look in mine,
           Peeping stars they seem to be.

Golden beams are shining, love,
Shining on you to bless;
Like the queen of night you fill
Darkest space with loveliness.
Silver stars how bright, love,
Mother moon in thronely might,
Gaze on us to bless, love,
Purest vows here made to night.

    Chorus: Twinkling stars are laughing love,
           Laughing on you and me;
           While your bright eyes look in mine,
           Peeping stars they seem to be.

JOHN P ORDWAY – 1855

Belle of Tennessee!
A Plantation Love Song

Dexter Smith wrote *Belle of Tennessee! A Plantation Love Song*.[10] Smith was born in Salem, Massachusetts, on November 14, 1837, and as a child, preferred reading to playing with other children. Dexter, not wanting to follow his father's pursuits was "determined to lead a mercantile life until he should find such a position in the field of literature." [11] It was written in the *Phrenological Journal and Packard's Monthly* that "One reason why his songs are so popular is that the spirit of his mind flows in harmony with that of common humanity like that of (Scottish poet Robert) Burns." [12]

Does the mockin' bird grow weary
Of his singin' to his dearie
As they nestle mid the
White magnolia plumes?
Does the oriole sing clearer
'cause his mate is hov'rin' nearer
When the night am fragrant
With summer blooms?

So my heart is singin' sweetly
As the daylight fades completely
For I know that you'll be
Waitin' up of me for me
When the moonbeams are a gleamin'
An the starlight am a streamin'
Then I'll meet you,
My Belle of Tennessee.

Chorus: Oh my honey! Life is sunny
For you are more precious more than gold to me;
Love me sweetie! Love your Petie!
For I love you, my Belle of Tennessee.

As we sit with arms entwinin',
While the big moon is a-shinin'
Both our hearts am fondly
Beatin' to one strain,
As the shafts from Luna's Quiver
Turn to silver on the river
Somethin' tells me life
Will never give us pain.

We will share our joys together,
Thro' life's fair or stormy weather
And the world shall be
Unending jubilee for me,
If what ever be beside me,
O! my darlin', my Belle of Tennessee.

Chorus: Oh my honey! Life is sunny
For you are more precious more than gold to me;
Love me sweetie! Love your Petie!
For I love you, my Belle of Tennessee.

DEXTER SMITH & N. HARRIS WARE – 1897

*Belle of Tennessee! A Plantation
Love Song,* from Author's
Personal Collection

WALNUT GROVE.   C. M.

~ 9 ~
Children Songs

Kid Do Go

William Wells Newell wrote in *The Passover Song of the Kid and an Equivalent from New England*, published in the *Journal of American Folklore*, about *Kid Do Go:* "I now print" he says "for the first time a version obtained by myself, many years ago, from the recitation of Miss Lydia R. Nichols of Salem, Massachusetts at the time aged 88 years, who retained the words as a reminiscence of her earliest infancy; the date of the rhyme therefore goes back to about 1800." [1]

As I was going over London Bridge,
I found a penny ha'penny, and bought me a kid.
    Kid do go.
Know by the moonlight it 's almost midnight,
Time kid and I were home an hour and a half ago.

Went a little further, and found a stick.
    Stick do beat kid, Kid won't go.
Know by the moonlight it 's almost midnight,
Time kid and I were home an hour and a half ago.

Went a little further, and found fire.
    Fire do burn stick,
    Stick won't beat kid, Kid won't go.
Know by the moonlight it 's almost midnight,
Time kid and I were home an hour and a half ago.

Went a little further, and found water.
    Water do quench fire,
    Fire won't burn stick,
    Stick won't beat kid, Kid won't go.
Know by the moonlight it 's almost midnight,
Time kid and I were home an hour and a half ago.

Went a little further, and found ox.
      Ox do drink water,
      Water won't quench fire,
      Fire won't burn stick,
      Stick won't beat kid, Kid won't go.
Know by the moonlight it 's almost midnight,
Time kid and I were home an hour and a half ago.

Went a little further, and found butcher.
      Butcher do kill ox,
      Ox won't drink water,
      Water won't quench fire,
      Fire won't burn stick,
      Stick won't beat kid, Kid won't go.
Know by the moonlight it 's almost midnight,
Time kid and I were home an hour and a half ago.

Went a little further, and found rope.
      Rope do hang butcher,
      Butcher won't kill ox,
      Ox won't drink water,
      Water won't quench fire,
      Fire won't burn stick,
      Stick won't beat kid, Kid won't go.
Know by the moonlight it 's almost midnight,
Time kid and I were home an hour and a half ago.

Rope began to hang butcher, butcher began to kill ox,
      Ox began to drink water,
      Water began to quench fire,
      Fire began to burn stick,
      Stick began to beat kid, Kid began to go.
Know by the moonlight it 's almost midnight,
So kid and I got home an hour and a half ago.

TRADITIONAL – 1800

The Cat and the Mouse

The Cat and the Mouse is from the recitation of Miss Lydia R. Nichols of Salem around 1800 and "represents the story as current in New England at the time of the earliest memory of the reciter." [2]

The cat and the mouse went into the oven together.
The cat bit off the mouse's tail,
And the mouse bit off the cat's thread.
The mouse said, " Aye gi' me my own tail again.

I won't without you go the cow and get me some milk.
    Titty mouse hop, and titty mouse run, to the cow I come.
Do cow gi' me milk, I give cat milk,
Cat gi' me my own tail again.

I won't without you go to the barn and get me some hay.
    Do titty mouse hop, and titty mouse run, to the barn I come.
Do barn gi' me hay,
I give cow hay, cow gi' me milk,
I give cat milk, cat gi' me my own tail again.

I won't without you go to the blacksmith and get me a lock and key.
    Titty mouse hop, and titty mouse run, to the blacksmith I come.
Do blacksmith gi' me lock and key,
I give barn lock and key, barn gi' me hay,
I give cow hay, cow gi' me milk,
I give cat milk, cat gi' me my own tail again.

I won't without you go to the sea and get me some coal.
    Titty mouse hop, and titty mouse run, to the sea I come.
Do sea gi' me coal,
I give blacksmith coal, blacksmith gi' me lock and key,

I give barn lock and key, barn gi' me hay,
I give cow hay, cow gi' me milk,
I give cat milk, cat gi' me my own tail again.
I won't without you go to the cock and get me a feather.
      Titty mouse hop, and titty mouse run, to the cock I come.
Do cock gi' me feather,
I give sea feather, sea gi' me coal,
I give black- smith coal, blacksmith gi' me lock and key,
I give barn lock and key, barn gi' me hay,
I give cow hay, cow gi' me milk,
I give cat milk, cat gi' me my own tail again.

I won't without you go to the miller and get me some corn.
      Titty mouse hop, and titty mouse run, to the miller I come.
Do miller gi' me corn,
I give cock corn, cock gi' me feather,
I give sea feather, sea gi' me coal,
I give blacksmith coal, blacksmith gi' me lock and key,
I give barn lock and key, barn gi' me hay,
I give cow hay, cow gi' me milk,
I give cat milk, cat gi' me my own tail again.

The miller gave him some corn, and he gave it to the cock,
The cock gave him a feather, and he gave it to the sea,
The sea gave him some coal, and he gave it to the blacksmith,
The blacksmith gave him a lock and key, and he gave it to the barn,
The barn gave him some hay, and he gave it to the cow,
The cow gave him some milk, and he gave it to the cat,
And the cat gave him his own tail again.
But after all his trouble,
      the tail was of no use
        to the poor mouse.

TRADITIONAL — 1800

Trot, Trot, to Boston

There are several variants to this children's play song. When singing *Trot, Trot to Boston* [4] with a young child on your knee, you bounce the child up and down like trotting on a horse. As the singing progresses, your knee bounces higher and higher until you collapse your knee, and the child pretends to fall off the horse. Additional, silly verses can be added or just made up.

> Trot, trot, to Boston;
> Trot, trot, to Lynn;
> Trot, trot, to Salem;
> Home, home again.

TRADITIONAL – UNKNOWN

Epitaph on a Favorite Pig

The *Epitaph on a Favorite Pig* [4] was found in the *Salem Gazette*. This song could have been sung to reminisce with children about the passing of their favorite pig.

> Ye dryads weep, ye nymphs bemoan,
> Warble your note in plaintive tone;
> Let every heart be sad;
>
> Ye chirping birds, your songs refrain,
> And join with me in mournful strain,
> Alas, my Piggy's dead!
> Cut off in bloom,
> Sent to the tomb,
> E'er half his days were run;
> Relentless death,

Has stop'd his breath,
My Pig's forever gone!

These sparkling eyes no more shall see
The dawning light, or pleasant day;
His mouth has shut sweet music's door,
And ughs and eeks are heard no more.
His antic tricks no more shall please,
His social chat is done;
Farewell, dear Pig; I ne'er will cease
They cruel fate to mourn,

While the stars roll round in spheres,
While the queen of night appears,
While the sun his course shall keep,
For little dear Piggy, I will weep.

TRADITIONAL – 1797

EPITAPH ON A FAVORITE PIG.

Ye dryades weep, ye nymphs bemoan,
Warble your notes in plantive tone;
Let every heart be sad;
Ye chirping birds, your songs refrain,
And join with me in mournful strain,
Alas, my Piggy's dead!
Cut off in bloom,
Sent to the tomb,
E'er half his days were run;
Relentless death,
Has stop'd his breath,
My Pig's for ever gone!
Those sparkling eyes no more shall see
The dawning light, or pleasant day;
His mouth has shut sweet music's door,
And ughs and eeks are heard no more.
His antic tricks no more shall please,
His social chat is done;
Farewel, dear Pig; I ne'er will cease
Thy cruel fate to mourn.
While the stars roll round in spheres,
While the queen of night appears,
While the sun his course shall keep,
For little dear Piggy, I will weep.

Epitaph on a Favorite Pig.
Salem Gazette, July 4,
1797 #619

KING ALCOHO
a Comic
Temperance Gle
Sung by the
HUTCHINSON FAMI
TUNE, "KING ANDREW"
BOSTON Published by OLIVER DITSON 135 W

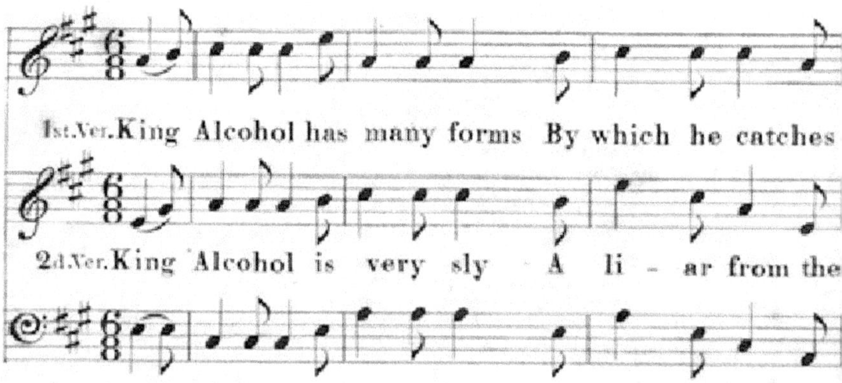
ALLEGRETTO.
1st. Ver. King Alcohol has many forms By which he catches
2d. Ver. King Alcohol is very sly A li - ar from the

~ 10 ~

Temperance

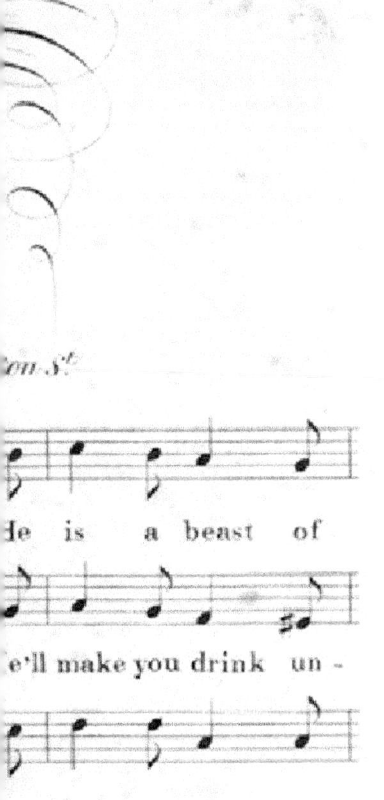

The Drunken Soldier

Drunken Soldier[1] was found in the *Salem Mercury* and is sung to the tune of *In a Mouldering Cave Where the Wretched Retreat*.

In a cottage forlorn, with a sigh and a pout,
   Poor T(r)im sat distracted with care;-
He look'd at his bottle, and saw it was out,
   And gave himself up to despair.

The walls of his cell were he spatted around,
   With the grog he had vomited up!
And even the dirt & the grass on the ground
   Were bestow'd with the dregs of his cup.

The housewife beheld thro a hole in the wall,
   Him weeping (his whisky half spent).
She cuss'd him, his liquor, his bottle and all,
   And these were the blessings she sent:

"O Trim do forbear, not a grunt nor a swear,
   For your grog, so deservedly lost,
Your home shall be broke; I will put up my prayer.
   And the answer shall be to your code.

The boys of the barracks, those soldiers so bold,
   Of gaming have finish'd their talk,
And such in the news, it is currently told-
   They are coming so drink out your stalk.

A council was held ere your eyes were awake,
    And this was the Captain's decree,
That when it is emptied the bottle shall break,
    And the charge they have trusted to me.

To the broomstick straightway, like a fury the flew;
    But he with his bottle began,
And said, that the door, let me touch it once more,
    And then, they may drink if they can.

With a circle of black the encompass'd his eyes;
    At last into slumbers he sunk,
Then they laid him down snug, left the sight of his jag
    Should tempt him again to get drunk.

TRADITIONAL – 1787

Father Mathew Statue Postcard,
courtesy of Sal Pangallo

King Alcohol (parody)

King Alcohol, [2] a temperance song sung by the Hutchinson Family, is a parody of the song *King Andrew* and sung to the tune of *Dame Durden*. Deacon Giles Distillery in Salem inspired the song, which is "a cautionary tale about making deals with demon rum. The story concerned a Salem deacon who ran a combination Bible manufactory and distillery." The distiller was supposed to make a deal with the devil to produce his rum, but his "mischievous workers burned his factory." [3]

King Alcohol has many forms,
By which he catches men
He is a beast of many horns,
And ever thus has been.

Chorus: For there's rum, and gin, and beer, and wine
And brandy of logwood hue
And hock, and port, and flip combined
To make a man look blue.
He says be merry, for here's good sherry
And Tom and Jerry, champagne and perry,
And spirits of every hue.

O are not these a fiendish crew
As ever a mortal knew.
O are not these a fiendish crew
As ever a mortal knew.

King Alcohol is very sly,
A liar from the first
He'll make you drink until you're dry,
Then drink because you thirst

King Alcohol has had his day,
His kingdom's crumbling fast
His votaries are heard to say,
Our tumbling days are past.

    Chorus: For there's rum, and gin, and beer, and wine
           And brandy of logwood hue
           And hock, and port, and flip combined
           To make a man look blue.
           He says be merry, for here's good sherry
           And Tom and Jerry, champagne and perry,
           And spirits of every hue.

           And now they are a temperate crew
           As ever a mortal knew.
           And now they are a temperate crew
           And have given the devil his due.

The shout of Washingtonians,
Is heard on every gale
They're chanting now the victory,
O'er cider, beer, and ale.

    Chorus: For there's rum, and gin, and beer, and wine
           And brandy of logwood hue
           And hock, and port, and flip combined
           To make a man look blue.
           He says be merry, for here's good sherry
           And Tom and Jerry, champagne and perry,
           And spirits of every hue.

           And now they are a temperate crew
           As ever a mortal knew.
           And now they are a temperate crew
           And have given the devil his due.

JESSE HUTCHINSON – 1850

A Parody

George B. Cheevers wrote *A Parody*, [4] located in the Broadside Collection at the Phillips Library. The original site of Deacon Giles' Distillery was on Front Street in Salem, and according to legend, "Deacon Giles inherited both the family distillery and a sense of piety. Unwilling to give up either because of the profit involved with the former and the respectability of the latter, he continued to make rum and enslave his workers with one hand and sell bibles with the other." [5] This broadside from 1835 details the temperance point of view.

In Salem, when the sun was low,
Deep silence held each street and row,
And solemn was the distant flow,
Of ocean rolling rapidly.

But Salem saw another sight,
When lurid fires and candle light,
Gleamed bluely out of the dead of night,
From Deacon Giles' Distillery.

And redder yet those fires shall glow,
At Salem's frighten street shall know,
When gibb ring friends their embers blow,
In Deacon Giles' Distillery.

The twilight deepens-come! ye brave,
Let loose from Hell (the Skeptic's grave,)
Your dusky plumes in triumph wave
Over Deacon Giles' Distillery.

Then rock'd the Still, with riot riven,
Then worked the fiends from Bible given:
And louder than fresh bolts from heaven,
Loud groaned the old distillery.

Tis morn- nor did you lurid sun,
Behold the fiends; their work is done;
Each clutched his book and out he run,
From Deacon Giles' Distillery.

They part, alas! Too soon to meet,
Their foreman, though and arrant cheat,
Ne'er leaves his business incomplete,
He works beyond the Sepulcher.

GEORGE B. CHEEVERS – 1835

A Water Song

A Water Song was written by George F. Chever of Salem and can be found in *The Family Fire-side Book or Monuments of Temperance*. [6] Rescue (temperance) songs were sung at the Old Jerry McAuley Mission in New York and at the Hadley Mission in Salem, Massachusetts. Evangelists throughout the United States sang these songs for temperance and enlightenment. The Hadley Mission was located on Central Street [7] in Salem and closed on October 31, 1898. [8]

COLD, crystal water to me bring,
Creation's wide and liquid wealth,
From out whose gushing fountain's spring
Eternal purity and health.

O! Who can count the precious worth,
Of such a boon to mortals given,
All other drinks are brewed on earth,
But water cometh down from Heaven.

Far in the clear, cold upper air,
The Spirits of God's holy will,
This calm, pure Earth-drink fit prepare,
And Heaven's unfailing fountains fill.

No soul e'er fell to it a prey,
No palsied of the mind or limb,
Can trembling point to it, and say,
"I drank my poison from its brim."

Then crystal water to us bring,
Creation's wide and liquid wealth,
From out whose gushing fountain's spring,
Eternal purity and health

GEORGE F. CHEVER – 1851

Chug's at Cabot Farm (Broadside)

The temperance movement in Salem was alive and well with The Hadley Rescue Mission, teetotalist Father Mathew's visit to Salem, the women's movement, the anti-slavery movement, and the Second Annual Picnic at Cabot Farm in North Salem on September 6, 1897. The broadside quote promoting the gathering: "Kosy Korners for all," and "Soft Drinks served by bewitching young damsels at the Pavilion," seemed to set the tone for the day. No information has been found on the Chug's Orchestra, but it was probably a local North

Shore band.[9] A notice titled, " *Guest at Cabot Farm*" published in the *Salem Gazette* on September 7, 1897 describes the occasion. "A number of Salem young people were entertained by Holton Jewett at his summer home at Cabot Farm yesterday afternoon."[10]

GUESTS AT CABOT FARM

A number of Salem young people were entertained by Helton Jewett at his summer home at Cabot Farm yesterday afternoon. A pleasant time was enjoyed on the lawn watching different games and in social conversation. Refreshments were served during the afternoon.

Salem Gazette, September 7, 1897

Second Annual Picnic at Cabot Farm, courtesy of Nancy Lutts

The Drunkard's Wish

The Drunkard's Wish [11] was found in the *Salem Gazette*. Sugar that was grown in the Caribbean was processed into molasses. Salem merchants imported the molasses and produced rum that had an excellent reputation throughout Salem and New England.

> Lovely Rum! Enchanting sound!
> So often fought, so often found-
> With New England from the still
> Let me know my gullet fill-
>
> This is all I wish to have,
> This is all I ask or grave-
> This will raise me from despair,
> And ease my mind of every year.
>
> When my spirits are quite low,
> This will make them briskly flow-
> This liquor it does so bewitch,
> When I'm poor it makes, me rich-
>
> When it does its joy impart,
> Light as feathers makes my heart-
> Lighter still it makes my head,
> When it's charming fumes are spread.
>
> Bacchanalians hither come,
> And all ye votaries of Rum-
> Come and join she jovial throngs,
> Rum inspires the cheerful song-

Liquor that will raise such mirth,
Sure is of celestial birth,
If a story thrice is told,
Let it be ne'er so old.

Take another glass or two,
Suit the story it is new.
Let me with the bottle live,
Nothing else can pleasure give.

This adds beauty to each grace,
Lively red it gives the face,
Gives the breath a rich perfume,
Sweeter than the rose of June.

Fragrant as the balmy fields,
Or the spice that India yields-
Give me courage when I talk,
Makes me run, when I can't walk.

Makes me with a proper spirit,
Resent the ills I do not merit,
Like the infant at the breast,
So it lulls me quite to rest.

'Till terrific Death shall come,
I shall ever sing of Rum,
When this groggy life I've past,
Let me turn to Rum at last.

TRADITIONAL – 1796

*The Drunkard's Wish, Salem
Gazette*, December 6, 1796, #557

THE DRUNKARD'S WISH

LOVELY Rum! enchanting sound!
Often fought, fo often found—
In New-England from the ftill—
Give me now my gullet fill—
This is all I afk or crave,
This will raife me from defpair,
This will raife my mind of every care,
And eafe my mind of every care,
When my fpirits are quite low,
This will make them brifkly flow.
This liquor it does fo bewitch,
When I'm poor it makes me rich—
When it does its joys impart,
Light as feathers makes my heart,
Lighter ftill it makes my head.
When its charming fumes are fpread.
Bacchanalians hither come,
And all ye votaries of Rum—
Come and join the jovial throng,
Rum infpires the chearful fong.
Liquor that will raife fuch mirth,
Sure is of celeftial birth.
If a ftory thrice is told,
Let it be ne'er fo old,
Take another glafs or two,
Suit the ftory if is new.
Let me with the bottle live,
Nothing elfe can pleafure give.
This adds beauty to each grace,
Lively red it gives the face,
Gives the breath a rich perfume,
Sweeter than the rofe in June,
Fragrant as the balmy fields,
Or the fpice that India yields—
Gives me courage when I talk,
Makes me run when I can't walk—
Makes me with a proper fpirit,
Refent the ills I do not merit.
Like the infant at the breaft,
So it lulls me quite to reft.
'Till terrific Death fhall come,
I fhall ever fing of Rum.
When this groggy life I've paft,
Let me turn to Rum at laft.

Address to a Jug of Rum

Address to a Jug of Rum was found in the *Salem Gazette*. Father Mathew was associated with the *Cork Total Abstinence Society*, which was a movement that began on April 10, 1838 in Ireland. [12] Father Mathew visited Salem in September 1849 and laid the groundwork for the development of the Salem chapter of *Father Mathew's Catholic Total Abstinence Society*, which was organized in 1875. The organization purchased the Tucker Estate located on 129 Essex Street in Salem for its headquarters in 1886. [13] A statue of Father Mathew was erected to honor him in 1887. The statue's original location was at the corner of Phenix Hall and Central Street in Salem and was later moved in 1916 to its current location to the end of Hawthorne Boulevard on Derby Street. There is also a monument of Father Mathew in the city of Philadelphia, a statue on St. Patrick's Street in Cork, Ireland, and another statue on O'Connell Street in Dublin, Ireland.

Father Mathew Statue, courtesy of Mary Barker

Address to a Jug of Rum

Here only by a cork control'd,
And slender walls of earthen mound,

In all the pomp of death repose
The seeds of many a bloody nose;

The chattering tongue, the horrid oath,
The fist for fighting nothing loth,

The passion, which no words can tame.
That bursts, like sulphur, into flame;

The nose carbuncled, glowing red,
The bloated eye, the broken head;

The tree that bears the deadly fruit
Of murder, maiming, and dispute;

As of that Innocence assails,
The images of gloomy jails,

The giddy thought, on mischief bent,
The midnight hour in riot spent!

All these within this jug appear,
And Jack, the hangman, in the rear!

TRADITIONAL – 1813

The Last Glass

The Last Glass was found in the Alcohol, Temperance & Prohibition broadside series at the Brown University Library. This quote was printed on one of the broadsides: "Since the above gay and festive youth swore off (alcohol), they purchased with their extra money a hat, a pair of cuff buttons, a set of shirt studs, and a billed shirt at Franklin's 99 Cent Store on Essex Street in Salem." [14]

No, thank you, not any to night, boys, for me,
I have drank my last glass, have had my last spree;
You may laugh in my face; you may sneer if you will,
But I've taken my pledge, and I'll keep it until,
I am laid in the churchyard and sleep 'neath the grass;
And your sneers cannot move me- I've drank my last glass.

Just look at my face, I am thirsty to day,
It is wrinkled and hollow, my hair is turned gray,
And the light of my eyes that once brilliantly shone,
And the bloom of my cheek both are vanished and gone.
I am young, but the furrows of sorrow and care,
Are stamped on a brow once with innocence fair.

Ere manhood its seal on my forehead had set,
(And I think of the past with undying regret,)
I was honored and loved by the good and the true,
Nor sorrow, nor shame, nor dishonor I knew.
But the tempter approached me-I yielded and fell,
And drank of the dark, damming poison of hell.

Since then I trod in the pathway of sin;
And bartered my soul to the demon of gin;
Have squandered my manhood in riotous glee,
While my parents, heart broken, abandoned by me,
Have gone down to the grave, filled with sorrow and shame,
With a sigh for the wretch who dishonored their name.

God's curse on the glass! Nevermore shall my lip
Of the fatal and soul burning beverage sip;
Too long has the fiend in my bosom held sway,
Henceforth and forever I spurn him away;
And never again shall the death dealing draught
By me, from this hour, with God's blessing be quaffed.

So good night boys, I thank you, no liquor for me;
I have drank my last glass, have had my last spree;
You may laugh in my face; you may sneer if you will,
But I've taken my pledge, and I'll keep it until
I am laid in the churchyard and sleep 'neath the grass;
And your sneers cannot move me I've drank my last glass.

TRADITIONAL – 1800

The Last Glass

No, thank you, not any to night, boys, for me,
I have drank my last glass, have had my last spree;
You may laugh in my face, you may sneer if you will,
But I've taken the pledge, and I'll keep it until
I am laid in the church yard and sleep 'neath the grass;
And your sneers cannot move me—I've drank my last
   glass.
Just look at my face, I am thirty to day,
It is wrinkled and hollow, my hair is turned gray,
And the light of my eye that once brilliantly shone,
And the bloom of my cheek both are vanished and gone.
I am young, but the furrows of sorrow and care,
Are stamped on a brow once with innocence fair.
Ere manhood its seal on my forehead had set,
(And I think of the past with undying regret,)
I was honored and loved by the good and the true,
Nor sorrow, nor shame, nor dishonor I knew.
But the tempter approached me—I yielded and fell,
And drank of the dark, damning poison of hell.
Since then I have trod in the pathway of sin;
And bartered my soul to the demon of gin;
Have squandered my manhood in riotous glee,
While my parents, heart broken, abandoned by me,
Have gone down to the grave, filled with sorrow and

The Last Glass, courtesy of
the Harris Broadside
Collection, John Hay Library,
Brown University

FREE FREE

HIGH GRADE
Natural Tone
TALKING and
SINGING
MACHINE
FREE

Call at our store and hear the specially prepared Records of Bands and other instrumental Music, Songs, Stories, Recitations, etc., and assure yourself that this is the best offered. You Buy Only the Records

THESE RECORDS ARE FAMOUS FOR THEIR TONE AND QUALITY

As a home entertainer it has no equal. The best talent in the country is brought right to your fireside to while away the long evenings with comical recitations and songs. Or you may wish to learn a song and what better instructor can you have than one of the peerless singers to phrase a song over and over again if need be. The possibilities of this wonderful machine for instruction and amusement are endless.

DESCRIPTION OF INSTRUMENT

THE CABINET—Made of heavy, solid oak throughout. Corner posts are made with fluted mouldings.

NICKLED TONE ARM—The latest triumph of scientific research, producing the largest volume and purest tone quality, eliminating the metalic scratch so common in the ordinary type of machine.

THE MOTOR—Of special strength and construction, unusually durable.

TURN TABLE—Ten-inch diameter, accomodating any size disc record.

STANDARD ANALYZING REPRODUCER (Sound Box)—Insuring the most perfect reproduction of any known sound; fitted with automatic needle clamp, permitting of the instant releasing or fastening of the needles.

SPEED REGULATOR—Permitting the ready adjustment of the speed to suit the individual fancy or requirements such as for music or speaking records.

FLOWER HORN—Seventeen inches in length, with a fifteen inch flared bell. Finished in a beautiful, deep, rich red enamel, and decorated with gold stripes.

One Standard Talking Machine with Handsome Flower Horn FREE to every customer whose Cash Purchases amount to **$25.00**

See and hear this wonderful instrument and learn how easily you can obtain one

One Machine to each Home

Outlet Clothing House

Men's and Boys' Clothing and Gents' Furnishing Goods.

17-19 FRONT ST.   Branch Store:—87 Lafayette St.

Salem   Massachusetts

Acknowledgments

I played my first Salem tune, the *Salem Artillery,* while playing stand-up bass in the Salem Country Orchestra. Over the next couple of years, the band added and continued playing Salem tunes like *Colonel Pickering's March to Lexington* and *Newhall's March.* Bill Smith, a Salem resident and folk musician who led the band, encouraged me to continue researching and compiling tunes and songs about Salem.

Since then, I have collected over 200 songs, ballads, and tunes and have included 68 of them in this book, *Old Salem in Ballad and Song.* They all have a connection to Salem with notes and references. A follow-up book of sea songs, ballads, and sea shanties called *Old Salem at Sea in Ballad and Song* is in the works.

I would like to thank my wife Jennifer for her support throughout this process, for her work at the Salem Public Library, and for developing the website Salem Links and Lore, a local source for Salem history, found on the Salem Public Library's website. I am particularity thankful to Bill and Sarah Smith, longtime friends, Salem residents, and folk musicians, for their continual encouragement and support with this project. Thank you to local historian, Jim McAllister for writing the foreword and for sharing his vast knowledge of Salem's history with the Salem community. Special thanks to Sal Pangallo, Jarlath MacNamara of the Athlone Community Radio, Ireland, Dee Dee Morneau, Jim Dalton, Joanna Liss, Christine Elizabeth Mistretta, Betsey and Ed Bennett and Nancy Lutts for the use of their private collections. Thank you to maritime photographer, Mary Barker for the use of her photographs of Salem, Gracie Arcand Sabean for editing and to my daughter, Rosie Strom for sharing her graphic design knowledge, suggestions, and talent.

I would also like to thank all the librarians and researchers for their knowledge and support at the following libraries: Historic Beverly, Boston Public Library, Center for Popular Music, Middle Tennessee State University, Library Company of Philadelphia, Library of Congress, the Harris Broadside Collection at the John Hay Library at Brown University, House of the Seven Gables, the Lester S. Levy Collection of Sheet Music, at Johns Hopkins University, The Philips Library at the Peabody Essex Museum in Rowley and Salem, the Frederick E. Berry Library at Salem State University, Salem Public Library, and the Washington University Digital Gateway Image Collections & Exhibitions.

Lastly, I would like to acknowledge all our music friends and local sessions for which we all share our love of music and community.

Enjoy Salem and keep singing - Bob Strom

Nautical photographer, **Mary Barker** specializes in candid environmental photography, documenting the restoration of the historic wooden fishing vessels, as well as capturing schooners and other tall ships both dockside and under sail. Mary is the resident documentarian for the *Schooner Adventure* and considered "one of our own" at Gloucester Marine Railways. Mary's nautical restoration photographs have been featured in *Wooden Boat*, *Marlinspike*, *Sea History Magazine,* and the *2018 Tall Ship Directory.*

Endnotes

INTRODUCTION

1. Harriet E. Peet, "English Composition in the Elementary School: Studies in Ballad Literature." *The School Journal, vol. 75* (New York: A. S. Barnes & Company, 1115 Last Twenty Fourth Street, vol. LXXV, 1907 and 1908), 574.
2. "Newburyport Fire Leads to Execution For Arson," retrieved online July 17, 2107, https://www.massmoments.org/moment-details/newburyport-fire-leads-to-execution-for-arson.html.
3. *The New England Blacking Man*, Kenneth S. Goldstein Collection of American Song Broadsides, Center for Popular Music, Middle Tennessee State University (Boston: Eldridge & Co. Wholesale Agents, Nos. 47 & 48 North Market Street, corner Merchants' Row, 1850 - 1880, retrieved online July 21, 2017, www.popular.music@mtsu.edu.
4. Redfern Mason, *The Song Lore of Ireland* (New York: Wessels & Bissell Co., 1910), 299.
5. Robert B. Waltz and David G. Engle, *When Johnny Comes Marching Home*, The Ballad Index, retrieved online February 14, 2019, www.fresnostate.edu/folklore/ballads/RJ19233.html.
6. Manuel Fenollosa and R. T. L., *Emancipation Hymn* (Boston: Oliver Ditson & Co., 1863).
7. Oliver Jenkins, *Open Shutters, a Volume of Poems* (Chicago: W. Ransom, 1922), 39.

1. SALEM

Under the Willows

1. Bob Franke, *Under The Willows, Brief Histories*, Flying Fish, FF-70495, 1992, CD.
2. Eleanor Putnam, *Old Salem* (Boston and New York: Houghton, Mifflin and Company, 1889), 64.

Ode To Salem (City of Peace)

3. Alice Osborne Atwood, *Pageant of Salem: Kernwood*, Official Program, Salem, Massachusetts, June 13, 14, 16 and 17, House of the Seven Gables, Settlement Association, 1913, 15.
4. "House of Seven Gables, Caroline Emmerton," retrieved on line January 20, 2019, https://7gables.org/history/caroline-emmerton/.

5. Duane Hamilton Hurd, *History of Essex County, Massachusetts with Biographical Sketches of Many of its Pioneers and Prominent Men, vol. 1, Issue 1* (Philadelphia, PA: J.W. Lewis & Co., 1888), 227.

6. Charles Charleton Coffin, ed., *Bay State Monthly, A New England Magazine of History, Biography, Literature and State Progress vol. III* (Boston: Boston Bay State Monthly Company), 1885, 304 & T. De Witt Talmage, D.D., ed., *Frank Leslie's Sunday Magazine vol. XVIII July – December 1885* (New York: Frank Leslie's Publishing House), 1885, 658.

The Origin of the "Salem Shag"

7. Huntress & Dennis Aylward, *The Origin of the "Salem Shag, Essex Institute Collection vol. XXXI* (Salem, Mass.: The Salem Press), 1894 - 95, 216.

To Cold Spring in North Salem

8. G.L. Streeter, "To Cold Spring in North Salem," *Historical Collection of the Essex Institute vol. 2* (Henry Whipple, Institute & Son, 1860), 6.

9. Rachel Valliere Duffalo, *The Lineage of the Goodell Family(s) of Westminster*, retrieved online January 2,2018, www.usgennet. org /usa/vt/town/ westminster/goodell.html.

10. Helen R., Deese, Ed., *The Complete Poems By Jones Very* (Athens & London: University of Georgia Press, 1993), 231.

Smoking - on 76 Chestnut Street

11. Ship *Ringleader* logbook, Log 1906, Phillips Library, Peabody Essex Museum, Rowley, MA

12. "Registry of Deeds," retrieved online November 13, 2108, www.salemdeeds.com

Observations of Their Travel

13. Thomas Belsham, *The Christian Pioneer Intended To Uphold The Great Doctrines of the Reformation*, vol. IV, September 1829 (Glasgow: James Hedderwick & Son, 1829), 239.

14. Roger Williams, *Observations of Their Travel*, retrieved online September 5, 2018, http://www.hymntime.com/tch/bio/w/i/l/l/williams_roger.htm, & Benedict Gagliardi and Armand Aromin, *The Ocean State Songster*, (Presentation, Pinewoods Camp, Plymouth, Massachusetts, August 2018).

Whatcheer or Roger Williams in Banishment

15. Job Durfee & Thomas Durfee, ed., *Whatcheer or Roger Williams in Banishment, Complete Works of the Hon. Job Durfee LL D1 Late Chief Justice of Rhode Island with a Memoir of the Author* (Providence: Gladding and Proud,

Boston: Charles C. Little and James Brown, 1849), xiv.

16. Rev. J. Lewis Diman, ed., *Publications of the Narragansett Club: Key into the Language of America,* vol. I (Providence, RI: Providence Press Co., 1866), 2.

Salem Hornpipe (On the Road to Salem)

17. Patrick Sky, ed., *Ryan's Mammoth Collection Fiddle Tunes* (Pacific, MO: MelBay Publication, 1995, originally published in Boston, 1883), 120 & *On The Road To Salem.* Patrick Gilmore. (Boston: G.P. Reed & Co., 1853).
18. Jim Dalton, "Gilmore's Road To Salem," *Salem Gazette*, June 3, 2010.

Salem Artillery

19. *The Salem Artillery,* Transcribed by T. William Smith, Essex Institute, circa 1980.

Be Salem Home

20. *Essex Register,* March 17, 1826.

2. DYING & TRAGEDY

Written on reading an account of the execution of Stephen M. Clark

1. Young man of Salem, *Lines written on reading an account of the execution of Stephen M. Clark,* Harris Broadsides. Brown Digital Repository, Brown University Library, retrieved online January 10, 2017 https://repository.library.brown.edu/studio/item/bdr:279434/.
2. *Account of the short life and ignominious death of Stephen Merrill Clark,* Salem [Mass.]: T.C. Cushing, 1821, Courtesy of Cornell University Law Library, Trial Pamphlets Collection, retrieved online January 10, 2017 http://reader.library.cornell.edu/docviewer/digital?id=sat:3908#page/1/mode/1up.
3. "Newburyport Fire leads to Execution For Arson," retrieved online July 17, 2107, www.mass moments.org/moment-details/newburyport-fire-leads-to-execution-for-arson.html.

George A. Brown

4. *Lines composed and sung at the grave of George A. Brown,* Kenneth S. Goldstein Collection of American Song Broadsides Center for Popular Music, Middle Tennessee State University, retrieved online July 18, 2017, http://popmusic.mtsu.edu.

A Funeral Elegy

5. *A Funeral Elegy,* occasioned by the tragedy, at Salem near Boston, on Thursday afternoon, the seventeenth of June, at which time the ten following persons, seven women and three men, were drowned, having been out on a party of pleasure, Pr. Salem, 1875, retrieved online July 18, 2017, Library of Congress, www.loc.gov/item/rbpe.03701700/.

6. Raymond H. Bates Jr., *Shipwrecks North of Boston, vol. I, Salem Bay* (Beverly, Massachusetts: Commonwealth Edition, 2000), 6.

Murder of Joseph White

7. *Murder of Joseph White* (1830), Harris Broadsides. Brown Digital Repository, Brown University Library, retrieved online July 27, 2017, https://repository library.brown.edu/studio/item/bdr: 281302/ & Robert Booth, *Death of an Empire, The Rise and Murderous Fall of Salem, America's Riches City* (New York: Thomas Dunne Books, St. Martin's Press, 2011).

Ballad of Giles Corey

8. John Allison, *Witches and War-Whoops: Early New England Ballads,* Folkways Records, FH5211, 1962, LP.

9. "Giles Corey & Goodwyfe Corey, A Ballad of 1692," *Bulletin of the Essex Institute, vol. I* (Salem, MA: Essex Institute Press, 1870), 15 & Samuel Drake, *The Witchcraft Delusion in New England, vol. V* (Roxbury, Mass.: Munsell Printers, 1865), 113 - 114.

Ring The Bell Softly

10. S.R. Wells, ed., *Phrenological Journal and Packard's Monthly* (New York: Samuel R. Wells, Publisher, 389 Broadway, 1870), 313.

11. S.R. Wells, ed., *Phrenological Journal and Packard's Monthly* (New York: Samuel R. Wells, Publisher, 389 Broadway, 1870), 313.

12. S.R. Wells, ed., *Phrenological Journal and Packard's Monthly* (New York: Samuel R. Wells, Publisher, 389 Broadway, 1870), 314.

13. Dexter Smith, *Dexter Smith Poems* (Boston: G. D. Russell & Company, 1868).

3. THE IMPRISONED

The Escape Of Old John Webb or Billy Broke Locks

1. Tom Drake, *Escape Of Old John Webb,* retrieved online July 18, 2017, www. lazyka.com/linernotes/thesongsEscapeofOldJohn.htm.

2. Barry Phillips, *British Ballads from Maine* As sung by Mrs. S.S. Thornton and Mrs. F.P. Barker of Maine (New Haven: Yale University Press, 1929) 393.
3. Burl Ives, *The Burl Ives Songbook* (New York: Ballantine Books, 1953), 28.
4. Alan Lomax, *The Folk Songs of North America* (New York: Doubleday & Company, 1960), 14.
5. Francis James Child, G. L. Kittredge, *The English and Scottish Popular Ballads* (Boston and New York: Houghton and Mifflin Company, Cambridge: The Riverside Press, 1904), 461.
6. *The Boston Evening Post*, Monday, October 16, 1738.

The Charlestown Land Shark

7. John Greenway, *American Songs of Protest* (Philadelphia: A.S. Barnes and Company, University of Pennsylvania Press, 1953), 25 & *Charlestown Land Shark* (1815) Harris Broadsides. Brown Digital Repository, Brown University Library, retrieved online July 18, 2017, https://repository.library.brown.edu/studio/item/bdr:267976/.

Susannah Martin

8. Wikipedia contributors, "Susannah Martin," Wikipedia, The Free Encyclopedia, retrieved online July 18, 2017, https://en.wikipedia.org/w/index.php?title=Susannah_Martin&oldid=875610689.
9. Diane Taraz, *A Silver Dagger ~ Exploring Women's History Through Folk Songs*, Raisin Pie Music RP-8, 2008, CD.
10. John Allison, *Witches and War-Whoops: Early New England Ballads,* Folkways Records, FH5211, 1962, LP.
11. John Greenleaf Whittier, *The Complete Poetical Works of John Greenleaf Whittier* (Cambridge: Houghton Mifflin Company, 1894), 64.

A lecture and a song concerning the Robbery at Newbury to some men in jail at Salem

12. Jonathan Plummer, *A lecture and a song, concerning the robbery at Newbury, to some men in jail at Salem,* Printed for the author, and sold by him. 1817, retrieved online July 18, 2017, https://www.loc.gov/resourcrbpe.05101400/.

4. SOCIAL CHANGE

Emancipation Hymn

1. Manuel Fenollosa and R. T L., *Emancipation Hymn*. Boston: Oliver Ditson & Co., 1863, Notated Music, retrieved online July 20, 2017, http://www.loc.gov/item/ihas.200001094/.

2. Heather Wilkinson Rojo, "Manuel Fenollosa, Spanish Immigrant to Salem, Massachusetts 1838," retrieved online July 20, 2017, www.genealogywise. com/profiles/blogs/manuel-fenollosa-spanish & *Emancipation Hymn*, Protest Song Lyrics, retrieved online July 20, 2017, www.protestsonglyrics. net/Freedom_Songs/Emancipation-Hymn.phtml.

Get Off the Track!

3. Jesse Hutchinson, *Get Off the Track* (Boston: Published by the Author, 1844), retrieved online, July 16, 2019, https://levysheetmusic.mse.jhu. edu/collection/012/156

4. "Music, Civil War," Americans at War, retrieved online July 20, 2017, https://www.encyclopedia.com/defense/energy-government-and-defense-magazines/music-civil-war.

5. "Popular Songs of the Day," retrieved online July 20, 2017, www.loc.gov/ collections/songs-of-america/articles-and-essays/musical-styles/popular-songs-of-the-day/.

6. Philip D. Jordan, *Singin' Yankees* (Minneapolis: The University of Minnesota Press, 1946), 96.

0 Thou To Whom in Ancient Time

7. George Barrett, B.A., ed., *Congregational Church Hymnal,* (London: Hodder and Stoughton, 27 Pateroster Row, 1887), 141.

8. Independent Congregational Church Papers, MSS 302, Phillips Library, Peabody Essex Museum, Salem, Mass.

9. Charles Dexter Cleveland & E.C. & J. Biddle, ed., *American Literature with Biographical Sketches and Selections From Their Work. A compendium of American literature*, No. 508 (Philadelphia, PA: Minor Street, 1862), 427 & "Charles Dexter Cleveland," retrieved online November 22, 2017, https://hymnary. org/person/Cleveland_CD3.

A Parting Hymn (Blessing)

10. Wikipedia contributors, "Charlotte Forten Grimké," Wikipedia, The Free Encyclopedia, retrieved January 16, 2019, https://en.wikipedia.org/w/ index.php?title=Charlotte_Forten_Grimk%C3%A9&oldid=851323627.

11. Brenda Stevenson, ed., *The Journals of Charlotte Forten* (New York: Oxford Press, 1988) & "Charlotte Forten," retrieved online January 15, 2019, https://www.salemstate.edu/charlotteforten.

12. *The Massachusetts Teacher and Journal of Home and School Education, Volume 9,* (Boston: Samuel Coolidge for the Massachusetts Teachers Association, 1856), 140.

Musical Entertainment at Mechanic Hall, Salem

13. *Musical Entertainment at Mechanic Hall, Salem* (Salem: Charles W. Swasey, Printer, 27 Washington Street, Salem, 1863).

14. Anne and Frank Warner, *Traditional American Folk Songs* (Syracuse University Press 1984), 357.

The Cornerstone Hymn

15. Lemuel Willis, *A Semi-centennial Address Delivered in the Universalist Church, Salem, Mass., Thursday August 4, 1859, on the Occasion of Celebrating the 50th Anniversary of the dedication of the Church* (Salem: Charles W. Swasey, Register Press, 1859), 66.

16. Amanda McGregor and Tom Dalton, "Universalist Church Celebrates 200th Birthday in Song," *Salem Evening News*, Friday, February 27, 2008.

5. CONFLICT

Departure of the Salem Light Infantry

1. *Departure of the Salem Light Infantry* (1861), Harris Broadsides Brown Digital Repository, Brown University Library, retrieved online August 9, 2017, https://repository.library.brown.edu/studio/item/bdr:270123/.

2. *5th Massachusetts Infantry* retrieved online August 9, 2017, www.firstbullrun.co.uk/NEV/Third%2Division/5th-massachusetts-infantry.html.

3. "Departure of Salem Troops," *The Salem Register*, April 23, 1861.

Lines written for the Second Reunion of the 23d Regiment

4. *Lines written for the Second Reunion of the 23d Regiment* from Kenneth S. Goldstein Collection of American Song Broadsides Center for Popular Music, Middle Tennessee State University, retrieved online July 18, 2017, http://popmusic.mtsu.edu.

5. Herbert E. Valentine, *Dedication of the boulder commemorating the service of the Twenty-third Regiment, Massachusetts Volunteer Infantry, in the Civil war, 1861-1865, at Salem, Massachusetts, September 28, 1905. United States Army. Massachusetts Infantry Regiment, 23rd (1861 - 1865)* (Salem: Newcomb & Gauss, Mass. 1905), 3.

When Johnny Comes Marching Home

6. Marwood Darlington, *Irish Orpheus, The Life of Patrick S. Gilmore Bandmaster Extraordinary* (Philadelphia: Oliver, Maney, Klien Co. 1950), 35.

7. Broadside ballad, *When Johnny Comes Marching Home*, retrieved online September 31, 2017, https://digital.nls.uk/broadsidesview/?id=16533.

8. Margaret Bradford Boni, *Fireside Book of Folk Songs* (New York: Simon and Schuster, 1947), 198.

9. Louis Charles Elson, *The National Music of America and its Sources* (Boston: L.C. Page and Company, 1900), 248.

10. Louis Lambert, *When Johnny Comes Marching Home Again*. Library of Congress, Washington, DC, 2002. retrieved online September 31, 2017. Library of Congress, https://www.loc.gov/item/ihas.200000024/.

Down on Manila's Bay

11. *Down on Manila's Bay.* Courtesy of Historic Beverly, www.historicbeverly.net.

12. *Salem Evening News,* September 2, 1898.

13. "City Pays Final Tribute to Medal of Honor Man Riley," *Salem Evening News,* November 18, 1950.

Ode of War and Washington

14. Wikipedia contributors, *War and Washington,* retrieved online September 31, 2017, https://en.wikipedia.org/wiki/War_and_ Washington.

15. Samuel Kettell, *Specimens of American poetry, with Critical and Biographical Notices, vol. 1* (Boston: S. G. Goodrich and Co., 1829), 198-199.

16. "Ode of War and Washington," *Salem Mercury,* Tuesday October 27, 1789, vol. III, #159.

17. Mary Caroline Crawford, *Little Pilgrimages Among Old New England Inns* (Boston: L.C. Page & Company, 1907, third Impression, 1908), 168.

Americans to Arms

18. "Poetry & Song on the Outbreak of War," retrieved online September 31, 2017, http://americainclass.org/sources/makingrevolution/crisis/text8/outbreakofwar.pdf.

Salem Mechanick Infantry Quick Step

19. Fitz Hugh Lane. *Salem Mechanick Infantry Quick Step* (Salem, Mass.: Ives & Putnam, 1836), retrieved online, July 16, 2019, https://levysheetmusic.mse.jhu.edu/collection/055/048.

Salem Independent Cadet Quick Step

20. Zetzsche, and S. Knaebel. *Salem Independent Cadet Quick Step* (Boston: Stephen W. Marsh, Boston, 1848), retrieved online, July 16, 2019, https://levysheetmusic.mse.jhu.edu/collection/084/003.

Original Ode: The First Shot of Freedom

21. City Authorities of Salem, *Memorial Services at the Centennial Anniversary of Leslie's Expedition to Salem* (Salem, Mass.: Salem Observer Printing Room 1875), 17.

The Original Ode

22. Oliver Ayer Roberts, *History of The Military Company of the Massachusetts, now called The Ancient and Honorable Artillery Company of Massachusetts, 1637-1888, vol. IV 1866-1888* (Boston: Alfred Mudge & Son Printers, 24 Franklin Street, 1901), 108.

Song of the Minute Man

23. George Rea Curwen and Ladies' Centennial Committee (Salem, Mass.), *Song of the Minute Man* (1875). Harris Broadsides, Brown Digital Repository, Brown University Library, retrieved online September 12, 2018, https://repository.library.brown.edu/studio/item/bdr:290807/.

Yankey Song

24. "Yankey Song," *Salem Gazette*, July 5, 1811.
25. Oliver Oldschool, *Port Folio vol. II,* (Philadelphia: John Watt, 1806), 123.

Salem Quick Step

26. Elias Howe, *The Musician's Companion* (Boston: Oliver Diston & Co., Washington Street Publication, 1842), 79 & John Jewett's, *National Flutina and Accordion Teacher: Complete Book of Instructions* (Boston: Oliver Diston & Co., Washington Street Publication, 1850), 36.

Salem Cadet's March

27. Elias Howe, *Howe's School for the Clarinet* (Boston: Oliver Diston & Co. Washington Street Publication, 1851), 21.

Colonel Pickering's March To Lexington aka Black Sloven

28. Louis Charles Elson, *The National Music of America and its Sources* (Boston: L.C. Page and Company, 1900), 146.
29. Allan Forbes, *Taverns and Stagecoaches of New England Anecdotes and Tales* (Boston: State Street Trust Company, 1953), 87.
30. Mary Harrod Northend, *We Visit Old Inn* (Boston: Murry Printing Company, Small Maynard & Co. 1925), 173.

31. John Warner Barber, *Historical Collections: Being a General Collection of Interesting Facts, Biographical Sketches, Anecdotes & co.* (Worcester: Warren Lasell, 1844), 175.

Dreaming of Home and Mother

32. John P. Ordway, *Dreaming of Home and Mother, ca. 1868.* retrieved online August 6, 2017, Photograph. https://www.loc.gov/item/2001701390/.
33. Oliver Ayer Roberts, *History of the Military Company of the Massachusetts, Now Called the Ancient and Honorable Artillery Company of Massachusetts, 1637-1888* (Boston: Alfred Mudge & Sons, Printer, 34 Franklin Street, 1901), 91.
34. J. Pierpont, and J Pierpont. *The One Horse Open Sleigh.* Oliver Ditson, Boston, monographic, 1857, Notated Music, retrieved online January 10, 2019, https://www.loc.gov/item/sm1857.620520/.

God Bless America

35. H. Leander D'Entremont, *God Bless America* a national anthem, H. Leander D'Entremont, Salem, Mass., 1919, retrieved online August 6, 2017, http://www.loc.gov/item/2013562539/.

6. COMMERCE

Our Ride to Lynn

1. J. C. Duchow, *Our Ride to Lynn,* The Phillip's Library Collection, Salem, 1850.

The First Trip

2. Francis C. Bradlee, *The Boston and Lowell Railroad* (Salem: Essex, Institute Collection, vol. LIV, Essex Institute, 1918), 222 - 223.

Hardware Advertisement

3. "Hardware Advertisement," *Salem Gazette,* July 11, 1800 #928.

The Irish Economy

4. "The Irish Economy," *Salem Gazette,* February 18, 1820.

Apprenticed in Salem

5. Peter Johnson and Friends, *Newport's Fair Town Traditional Songs and Ballads of North America.*, Living Folk Records, LFR 013, Living Folk, 2007, CD.
6. Broadside Collection, Bodleian Libraries and the Bodleian's digital Collections of Ballads, Oxford University, retrieved online October 20, 2018, http://ballads.bodleian.ox.ac.uk/search/printer/Hillatt%2C%20I.

The New England Blacking Man

7. *The New England Blacking Man* from Kenneth S. Goldstein Collection of American Song Broadsides, Center for Popular Music, Middle Tennessee State University, retrieved online July 21, 2017, http://popmusic.mtsu.edu/.

7. DANCING

1. Milton Gerald Hehr, *Musical Activities in Salem, Massachusetts*, 1783 - 1823, Ph.D. dissertation, Boston University, 1963, 87.
2. Milton Gerald Hehr, *Musical Activities in Salem, Massachusetts*, 1783 - 1823, Ph.D. dissertation, Boston University, 1963, 88.
3. F.E. Oliver, ed. *The Dairy of Benjamin Lynde and Benjamin Lynde, Jr.* (Boston: 1880), 48.
4. Mrs. Mary (Vail) Holyoke, *The Holyoke Diaries 1709 - 1856* (Salem Mass.: The Essex Institute), 48 - 106.

To a LADY who admired dancing

5. "To a LADY who admired dancing," *Salem Mercury*, July 29, 1788.
6. Milton Gerald Hehr, *Musical Activities in Salem, Massachusetts*, 1783 - 1823, Ph.D. dissertation, Boston University, 1963, 90.
7. Robert Rantoul, *A Historic Ball Room* (Salem, Mass.: The Essex institute Historical Collection vol. XXXI #7 & 12, 1894), 69.
8. Milton Gerald Hehr, *Musical Activities in Salem, Massachusetts*, 1783 - 1823, Ph.D. dissertation, Boston University, 1963, 90 & Essex Gazette May 31, 1774.
9. Jim McAllister, *Hamilton Hall, 1805*, Salem Tales, August 11, 2008, retrieved online June 16, 2017, www.salemweb.com.

The Flirtation

10. "The Flirtation," *Salem Gazette*, May 30, 1788.

Newhall's March
11. *Newhall's March,* Transcribed by Fred Finkle, source and date unknown.

Lailson's Ride
12. *Lailson's Ride,* Transcribed by T. William Smith circa 1980 from the manuscript collection at the Phillips Library & Elias Howe, *The Musician's Companion* (Boston: Oliver Diston & Co. Washington Street Publication, 1842), 54,

The Maid With Elbows Bare
13. "The Maid With Elbows Bare," *Salem Gazette,* #1223, May 17, 1803.

Chestnut Street
14. Hamilton Hall, retrieved online September 15, 2019, https://www.hamiltonhall.org/history.
15. H. K. Oliver, S. P. Tuckerman, S. A. Bancroft, *The National Lyre: A New Collection of Sacred Music, consisting of Psalm and Hymn Tunes, with a choice selection of Sentences, Anthems, and Chants* (Boston: Wilkins, Carter and Co. 1848), 54.

A New Song
16. M. C. D. Silsbee, *A Half Century in Salem* (Boston and New York: Houghton Mifflin & Co. The Riverside Press, Cambridge, 1887), i.
17. M. C. D. Silsbee, *A Half Century in Salem* (Boston and New York: Houghton Mifflin & Co. The Riverside Press, Cambridge, 1887), 88.
18. M. C. D. Silsbee, *A Half Century in Salem* (Boston and New York: Houghton Mifflin & Co. The Riverside Press, Cambridge, 1887), 88.
19. M. C. D. Silsbee, *A Half Century in Salem* (Boston and New York: Houghton Mifflin & Co. The Riverside Press, Cambridge, 1887), 91.

Pop Goes The Weasel
20. Fred A. Gannon, *Old Salem Scrap Book ll* (Salem, Mass.: Newcomb & Gauss in City Hall Square, for the Salem Book Co., M.F. McGrath), 21.
21. James M. Volo & Dorothy D. Volo, *Family Life in Seventeenth and Eighteenth Century America* (Westport CT: Greenwood Press, 2006), 264.
22. Opie and Opie, P., *The Singing Game* (Oxford: Oxford University Press, 1985), 217.

Dancing Instruction

23. M. C. D. Silsbee, *A Half Century in Salem* (Boston and New York: Houghton Mifflin & Co. The Riverside Press, Cambridge, 1887), 4.

24. The Annuals Festival, *Henry Upton's Afternoon Dancing School* (Salem: W. Harvey Merrill, Bookseller and Stationer), 1895.

Pyncheon Lane Capric

25. Charles Bancroft, *Illustrated history of Salem and environs: Souvenir edition of the Salem Evening News* (Salem, Mass.: Salem Evening News, 1897), 97.

26. Ryan Conary, David Moffat, Everett Philbrook, *House of the Seven Gables*, for the House of the Seven Gables Settlement Association (Charleston, South Carolina: Arcadia Publishing, 2017), 18 and 36.

Salem Willows For Mine

27. Rachel Zoll, "Salem Memorabilia Hunter Uncovers Willows Waltz," *Salem Evening News*. Monday May 1, 1995, 1.

28. Lou Collin, George Harry, *Salem Willows for Mine Waltz* (Salem, Mass.: L.A. Collins, Publisher, 1919).

Salem Country Dance (flyer)

29. Salem Country Dance Flyer, Self published by Chris Green, 1982.

30. Commonwealth Vintage Dancers. Fezziwig's Ball at Old Town Hall Salem, retrieved online September 28, 2019   http://vintagedancers.org

31. Hamilton Hall, The Resistance Ball, retrieved online September 28, 2019 www.hamiltonhall.org/events

High Street

32. T. William Smith, *High Street, Strawberry Jam,* Salem: Wellspring Studio, 2012, CD.

8. COURTSHIP

When I Saw Sweet Nellie Home

1. John Fletcher, *When I Saw Sweet Nellie Home* (Macon & Savannah: John C. Schreiner & Son, 1861), retrieved online December 2, 2017, https://www.loc.gov/item/ihas.200002502/.

2. *Seeing Nellie Home,* retrieved online December 2, 2017, www.fresnostate.edu/folklore/ballads/RJ19229.html.

3. Nicholas E. Tawa, *Arthur Foote: A Musician in the Frame of Time and Place* (Lanham, Maryland: Scarecrow Press, Inc., 1997), 45.

4. Wikipedia contributors, "Arthur Foote," Wikipedia, The Free Encyclopedia, retrieved online December 2, 2017, https://en.wikipedia.org/wiki/Arthur_Foote.

Seeing Nellie Home

5. Fred A. Gannon, *Old Salem Scrap Book* (Salem, Mass.: Newcomb & Gauss in City Hall Square, the Salem Book Co., M.F. McGrath, No copyright date given), 22.

6. The Walton's *The Quilting Soundtrack*, Season 4, Episode 22, February 12, 1976, retrieved online December 2, 2017, www.imdb.com/title/tt0743816/soundtrack.

7. Sarfraz Manzoor, *Scottish Roots of Johnny Cash, the man in black tartan*, retrieved online December 2, 2017, www.theguardian.com/music/2010/feb/07/johnny-cash-scottish-roots.

8. Rosanne Cash, *Time Travel and the Ballad Tradition* opinionator.blogs, retrieved online December 2, 2017, nytimes.com/2014/02/07/time-travel-and-the-balladtradition/?mcubz=3.

Twinkling Stars Are Laughing Love

9. John P. Ordway, *Twinkling Stars Are Laughing Love.* (Boston: J.P. Ordway, Ordway Hall, Washington Street, 1855), retrieved online October 1, 2019, http://levysheetmusic.mse.jhu.edu/collection/023/071.

Belle of Tennessee! A Plantation Love Song

10. Dexter Ware Smith, N. Harris, *Belle of Tennessee A Plantation Love Song* (Boston: Ent. Sta. Hall, 1897).

11. S.R. Wells, ed., *Phrenological Journal and Packard's Monthly* (New York: Samuel R. Wells, Publisher, 389 Broadway, 1870), 313.

12. S.R. Wells, ed., *Phrenological Journal and Packard's Monthly* (New York: Samuel R. Wells, Publisher, 389 Broadway, 1870), 311.

9. CHILDREN SONGS

Kid Do Go

1. William Wells Newell, *The Passover Song of the Kid and an Equivalent from New England,* The Journal of American Folklore, vol. 18, no. 68 (1905): 35-36. JSTOR, retrieved online September 17, 2017, www.jstor.orgstable/534260.

The Cat and the Mouse

2. *The Cat and the Mouse,* The Journal of American Folklore, vol. 13, no. 50 (July-Sept. 1900): 229. JSTOR, retrieved online September 17, 2018, www.jstor.org stable/534260 & William Bernard McCarthy, ed., *Cinderella in America: A Book of Folk and Fairy Tales,* (Mississippi: University Press, 2007), 57-58.

Trot, Trot to Boston

3. "Traditional Children's Songs & Nursery Rhymes," *Trot, Trot to Boston,* retrieved online September 17, 2017, www.traditionalmusic.co.uk/ childrens-songs/Trot_trot_to_Boston.htm.

Epitaph on a Favorite Pig

4. "Epitaph on a Favorite Pig," *Salem Gazette,* July 4, 1797 #619.

10. TEMPERANCE

The Drunken Soldier

1. "Drunken Soldier," *Salem Mercury,* Tuesday, September 25, 1787, #50.

King Alcohol, A Parody

2. John Wallace Hutchinson, *Story of the Hutchinson's (tribe of Jesse)* (Boston: Lee and Shepard, No. 10 Milk Street, 1896), 42.
3. Brian Roberts, *Blackface Nation: Race, Reform, and Identity in American Popular Music, 1812 - 1925* (Chicago: University of Chicago Press, 2017), 155.

A Parody

4. George B. Cheever, *A Parody, Alcohol, Temperance & Prohibition* (New York: J.S. Redfield, 1835), Phillips Library broadside collection.
5. Dale Cockrell, *Excelsior: Journals of the Hutchinson Family Singers, 1842 - 1846* (New York: Pendragon Press, 1989), 109.

A Water Song

6. Edward Cornelius Delavan, *The Family Fire-side Book or Monuments of Temperance, Containing: Temperance, Tales, Biography Sketches, Poetry, Essays Pleasing Instructive and Amusing* (Philadelphia: Leary & Getz, Publishers, 1853), 201.

7. City Documents for 1892 (Salem: Salem Observer Book and Job Print, 1893), 72.
8. Henry M. Meek, *The Naumkeag Directory for Salem, Beverly, Danvers, Marblehead, Peabody, Essex and Manchester* (Salem, Mass.: Henry M. Meek Publishing Company, 1898), 98.

Chug's at Cabot Farm (Broadside)

9. Second Annual Picnic at Cabot Farm from the collection of Nancy Lutts.
10. "Guests at Cabot Farm," *Salem Gazette*, September 7, 1897.

The Drunkard's Wish

11. "The Drunkard's Wish," *Salem Gazette*, December 6, 1796, #557.

Address to a Jug of Rum

12. Wikipedia contributors, "Father Mathew," Wikipedia, The Free Encyclopedia, retrieved online July 27, 2018, https://en.wikipedia.org/wiki/TheobaldMathew_%28temperance_reformer%29.
13. Father Mathew, retrieved online July 27, 2018 http://www.noblenet.org/salem/wiki/index.php/Father_Mathew Wiki source, Salem Links and Lore.

The Last Glass

14. *The Last Glass* (1860). Alcohol, Temperance & Prohibition, Brown Digital Repository, Brown University Library, retrieved online August 2, 2017, https://repository.library.brown.edu/studio/item/bdr:30273/.

Bibliography

Account of the short life and ignominious death of Stephen Merrill Clark, Salem, Mass.: T.C. Cushing, 1821.

Allison, John, *Witches and War-Whoops: Early New England Ballads*, Folkways Records, FH5211, 1962, LP.

Atwood, Alice Osborne, *Pageant of Salem: Kernwood*, Official Program, Kernwood, Salem, Massachusetts, June 13, 14, 16 and 17, House of the Seven Gables, Settlement Association, 1913.

Atlas of the City of Salem, Massachusetts. Philadelphia: G.M. Hopkins & Co., 1874.

Aylward, Huntress & Dennis. *The Origin of the "Salem Shag".* Essex Institute Collection Vol. XXXI. Salem, Mass.: The Salem Press, 1894 - 95.

Ballou, Hosea. *The Cornerstone Hymn.* Unknown Publisher, 1809.

Baltzell, Isiah. *Excerpt from Gates of Praise: For the Sabbath-School, Praise-Service, Prayer-Meeting, Etc.* Dayton, OH: W. J. Shuey, 1884.

Bancroft, Charles. *Illustrated history of Salem and environs:* Souvenir edition of the Salem Evening News. Salem, Mass.: Salem Evening News, 1897.

Bancroft, S. A., Oliver, H. K., Tuckerman, S. P. *The National Lyre: A New Collection of Sacred Music, consisting of Psalm and Hymn Tunes, with a choice selection of Sentences, Anthems, and Chants.* Boston: Wilkins, Carter and Co., 1848.

Barber, John Warner. *Historical Collections: Being a General Collection of Interesting Facts, biographical Sketches, Anecdotes & Relating to the History and Antiquities of Every Town in Massachusetts.* Worcester: Warren Lazell, 1844.

Barrett, George, B.A., ed., *Congregational Church Hymnal.* London: Hodder and Stoughton, 27 Pateroster Row, 1887.

Bates Raymond H., Jr., *Shipwrecks North of Boston, Volume I, Salem Bay.* Beverly, Massachusetts: Commonwealth Edition, 2000.

Belsham, Thomas. *The Christian Pioneer Intended To Uphold The Great Doctrines of the Reformation,* Vol. IV. September 1829. Glasgow: James Hedderwick & Son, 1829.

Boni, Margaret Bradford. *Fireside Book of Folk Songs.* New York: Simon and Schuster, 1947.

Booth, Robert, *Death of an Empire, The Rise and Murderous Fall of Salem, America's Riches City.* New York: Thomas Dunne Books, St. Martin's Press, 2011.

Bradlee, Francis C. *The Boston and Lowell Railroad.* Essex Institute Collection, Vol. LIV, Essex Institute, Salem, 1918.

Braithwaite, William Stanley ed., *Anthology of Magazine Verse for 1921.* Boston: Small, Maynard & Company, 1921.

Braithwaite, William Stanley ed., *Yearbook of American Poetry.* Boston: Small, Maynard & Company, 1921.

Brooks, Henry M. *The Olden Time Series, Vol. 6: Literary Curiosities - Gleanings Chiefly from Old Newspapers of Boston and Salem, Massachusetts.* Boston: Ticknor and Company, 1886.

Burzynski, Don. *The First Leathernecks: A Combat History of the U.S. Marines from Inception to the Halls of Montezuma.* Open Road Media, 2013.

Cheever, George B. *A Parody.* New York: J.S. Redfield, 1835.

Childs, Francis James. *English and Scottish Popular Ballads.* Edited from the collection of Francis James Child by Helen Child Sargent and George Lyman Kittredge. Boston and New York: Houghton Mifflin Company, Cambridge: The Riverside Press, 1904.

City Authorities of Salem, *Memorial Services at the Centennial Anniversary of Leslie's Expedition to Salem.* Salem, Mass.: Salem Observer Printing Room, 1875.

City Documents for 1892. Salem: Salem Observer Book and Job Print, 1893.

Cleveland, Charles Dexter & Biddle, E.C. & J. arranged and edited by, *American Literature with Biographical Sketches and Selections From Their Work. A compendium of American literature.* Philadelphia, PA: No. 508 Minor Street, 1862.

Cockrell, Dale. *Excelsior: Journals of the Hutchinson Family Singers, 1842 - 1846.* Stuyvesant, New York: Pendragon Press, 1989.

Coffin, Charles Charleton, ed., *Bay State Monthly, A New England Magazine of History, Biography, Literature and State Progress Volume III.* Boston: Boston Bay State Monthly Company, 43 Milk Street Boston, 1885.

Cole's Thousand Fiddle Tunes. Chicago, IL: M. M. Cole Publishing Co., 1967.

Collins, Lou and Harry, George. *Salem Willows for Mine Waltz.* Salem, Mass.: L.A. Collins, Publisher, 1919.

Conary, Ryan, Moffat, David, Philbrook, Everett. *House of the Seven Gables,* for the House of the Seven Gables Settlement Association. Charleston, South Carolina: Arcadia Publishing, 2017.

Crawford, Mary Caroline. *Little Pilgrimages Among Old New England Inns.* Boston: L.C. Page & Company, 1907, third Impression, November 1908.

Darlington, Marwood. *Irish Orpheus, The Life of Patrick S. Gilmore Band Extraordinary.* Philadelphia: Oliver, Maney, Klien Co., 1950.

Delavan, Edward Cornelius, *The Family Fire-side Book or Monuments of Temperance, Containing: Temperance, Tales, Biography Sketches, Poetry, Essays Pleasing Instructive and Amusing,* Philadelphia: Leary & Getz, Publishers, 1853.

Deese, Helen R., edited. *The Complete Poems By Jones Very.* Athens & London: The University of Georgia Press, 1993.

Diman, Rev. J. Lewis, editor. *Publications of the Narragansett Club: Key into the language of America Volume I.* Providence, RI: Providence Press Co., Printers, 1866.

Drake, Samuel. *The Witchcraft Delusion in New England*, Vol. V. Roxbury, Mass.: Munsell Printers, 1865.

Duchow, J. C. *Our Ride to Lynn*. Broadside Collection at The Phillip's Library Collection. Salem: No publisher given, 1850.

Durfee, Job, Durfee, Thomas, editor. *Whatcheer or Roger Williams in Banishment, Complete Works of the Hon. Job Durfee LL D1 Late Chief Justice of Rhode Island with a Memoir of the Author*. Providence: Gladding and Proud, Boston: Charles C. Little and James Brown, 1849.

Elson, Louis Charles. *The National Music of America and its Sources*. Boston: L.C. Page and Company, 1900.

Forbes, Allan. *Taverns and Stagecoaches of New England Anecdotes and Tales*. Boston: State Street Trust Company, 1953.

Forbes, Allan, & Eastman, Ralph M. *Taverns and Stagecoaches of New England Volume II*. Boston: State Street Trust Company, 1954.

Forbes, Allan and Eastman, Ralph M., *Town and City Seals of Massachusetts*, Boston: State Street Trust Company, 1950.

Franke, Bob. *Under The Willows, Brief Histories*. Flying Fish, FF-70495, 1992, CD.

Gagliardi, Benedict and Aromin, Armand. *The Ocean State Songster*. Providence, RI: Self-published by Gagliardi & Aromin, 2018.

Gannon, Fred A. *Old Salem Scrap Book*. Salem, Mass.: Newcomb & Gauss in City Hall Square, Salem Book Co., M.F. McGrath, No copyright date given.

Gannon, Fred A. *Old Salem Scrap Book II*. Salem, Mass.: Newcomb & Gauss in City Hall Square, Salem Book Co., M.F. McGrath. No copyright date given.

Greenway, John. *American Songs of Protest*. Philadelphia: A.S. Barnes and Company Inc., University of Pennsylvania Press, 1953.

Hadley; Henry Harrison. *National Christian Men's Temperance Union*. New York: H.H. Hadley, 1896.

Hehr, Milton Gerald. *Musical Activities in Salem, Massachusetts, 1783 - 1823*. Ph.D. diss., Boston University, 1963.

Holyoke, Mrs. Mary (Vail). *The Holyoke Diaries 1709-1856*. The Essex Institute, Salem Mass. No copyright date given.

Howe, Elias. *The Musician's Companion*. Boston: Oliver Diston & Co., Washington Street Publication, 1842.

Howe, Elias. *Howe's School for the Clarinet*. Boston: Oliver Diston & Co., Washington Street Publication, 1851.

Hurd, Duane Hamilton. *History of Essex County, Massachusetts with Biographical Sketches of Many of its Pioneers and Prominent Men, Vol. I, Issue 1*. Philadelphia, PA: J.W. Lewis & Co., 1888.

Hutchinson, Jesse. *Get Off the Track*. Boston: Published by the Author, 1844.

Hutchinson, Jesse. *King Alcohol, a Temperance Glee*. Boston: Oliver Diston, 135 Washington Street, 1843.

Hutchinson, John Wallace. *Story of the Hutchinson's (tribe of Jesse)*. Boston: Lee and Shepard, Publisher, No. 10 Milk Street, 1896.

Independent Congregational Church Papers, MSS 302, Phillips Library, Peabody Essex Museum, Salem, Mass.

Ives, Burl. *The Burl Ives Songbook*. New York: Ballantine Books, 1953.

Jenkins, Oliver. *Open Shutters, a Volume of Poems*. Chicago: W. Ransom, 1922.

Jewett, John. *Jewett's, National Flutina and Accordion Teacher: Complete Book of Instructions*. Boston: Oliver Diston & Co., Washington Street Publication, 1850.

Johnson, Peter and Friends. *Newport's Fair Town Traditional Songs and Ballads of North America*. Living Folk Records, LFR 013, Living Folk, 2007, CD.

Jordan, Philip D. *Singin' Yankees*. Minneapolis, Minnesota: The University of Minnesota Press, 1946.

Kettell, Samuel. *Specimens of American Poetry, with Critical and Biographical Notices, Vol. I*. Boston: S. G. Goodrich and Co., 1829.

Kuntz, Andrew. "Oh Ned!" *Fiddler Magazine*. North Sydney, N.S. Canada: Mary E. Larsen, Winter 2003/2004, vol.10, No. 4.

Langille, Claudine. Touchstone. *The New Land*. Green Linnet SIF 1040, 1982, LP.

Ship *Ringleader* logbook, Log 1906, Phillips Library, Peabody Essex Museum, Rowley, MA

Lomax, Alan. *The Folk Songs of North America*. Garden City, New York: Doubleday & Company, 1960.

Loring, George Bailey. *Celebration at North Bridge, Salem, July 4th, 1862: Oration*. Boston: J.E. Farwell & Company, 1862.

Mason, Redfern. *The Song Lore of Ireland*. New York: Wessels & Bissell Co., 1910.

Mason, Lowell. *Carmina Sacra: or, Boston Collection of Church Music: comprising the most popular psalm and hymn tunes in eternal use together with a great variety of new tunes, chants, sentences, motetts*. Boston: J. H. Wilkins & R. B. Carter, 1841.

Massachusetts Teacher and Journal of Home and School Education, Vol. 9. Boston: Samuel Coolidge for the Massachusetts Teachers Association, 1856.

McCarty, William, ed. *The American National Song-Book, Songs, Odes, and Other Poems, on National Subjects;* Compiled from Various Sources by Wm. McCarty. Philadelphia: Wm. McCarty, 1842.

McCarthy, William Bernard, ed. *Cinderella in America: A Book of Folk and Fairy Tales*. Jackson, Mississippi: University Press of Mississippi, 2007.

Meek, Henry M., Compiled by, *The Naumkeag Directory for Salem, Beverly, Danvers, Marblehead, Peabody, Essex and Manchester.* Salem, Mass.: The Henry M. Meek Publishing Company, 1898.

Missud, Jean M. *Salem Assemblies Waltzes.* Ditson & Co., Oliver, Boston, monographic, 1878.

Musical Entertainment at Mechanic Hall Salem. Salem: Charles W. Swasey, Printer, 27 Washington Street, Salem, 1863.

Northend, Mary Harrod. *We Visit Old Inn.* Boston: Murry Printing Company, Small Maynard & Co., 1925.

Nutter, Charles S. & Wilbur F. Tillett. *The Hymns and Hymn Writers of the Church.* New York: Methodist Book Concern, 1911.

Oldschool, Oliver. *The Port Folio Vol. II.* Philadelphia: John Watt, Publisher, 1806.

Oliver, F.E., ed. *The Dairy of Benjamin Lynde and Benjamin Lynde, Jr.* Boston: Privately Printed, 1880.

Opie and Opie, P. *The Singing Game.* Oxford: New York: Oxford University Press, 1985.

Ordway, John P. *Dreaming of Home And Mother.* Boston: Oliver Ditson & Co., 1865

Ordway, John P. *Twinkling Stars Are Laughing Love.* Boston: J.P. Ordway, Ordway Hall, Washington Street. 1855.

Peet, Harriet E. *The School Journal, Volume 75.* New York: A. S. Barnes & Company, 1115 Last Twenty Fourth Street, Vol. LXXV, 1907 and 1908.

Phillips, Barry. *British Ballads from Maine As sung by* Mrs. S.S. Thornton and Mrs. F.P. Barker of Maine. New Haven: Yale University Press, 1929.

Pierpont, J, and J Pierpont. *The One Horse Open Sleigh.* Oliver Ditson, Boston: monographic, 1857.

Putnam, Eleanor. *Old Salem.* Boston and New York: Houghton, Mifflin and Company, 1889.

Rantoul, Robert. "A Historic Ball Room." *The Essex institute Historical Collection Vol. XXXI #7 & 12*, Salem, Mass.: Essex Institute, 1894.

Roberts, Brian. B*lackface Nation: Race, Reform, and Identity in American Popular Music, 1812 - 1925.* Chicago: The University of Chicago Press, 2017.

Roberts, Oliver Ayer. *History of The Military Company of the Massachusetts, Now Called The Ancient and Honorable Artillery Company of Massachusetts, 1637-1888,* Vol. IV 1866 - 1888. Boston: Alfred Mudge & Son, 24 Franklin Street, 1901.

Ropes, Miss Lydia Nichols. *Narrating Facts Given to Her by Her Father, George Nichols.* Salem Mass.: The Salem Press Co., No copyright date.

Ryan, William Bradbury. *Ryan's Mammoth Collection: 1050 Reels and Jigs.* Boston: Elias Howe, 1883.

Salem Mechanick Light Infantry Quick Step. Arranged and Adapted by John
 Holloway. Salem, Mass.: Ives & Putnam, 1836.
*Seventeenth Annual Report of the Bureau of Statistics of Labor, Massachusetts Bureau of
 Statistics of Labor.* Boston: Wright & Potter Printing Co., 1886.
Silsbee, M. C. D. *A Half Century in Salem.* Boston and New York: Houghton
 Mifflin & Co. The Riverside Press, Cambridge, 1887.
Sky, Patrick. ed. *Ryan's Mammoth Collection Fiddle Tunes.* Pacific, MO:
 MelBay Publication, 1995.
Smith, Dexter. *Dexter Smith Poems.* Boston: G. D. Russell & Company, 1868.
Smith-Dalton. Maggie. *Stories and Shadows from Salem's Past.* Charleston and
 London: The History Press, 2010.
Smith, T. William. *High Street, Strawberry Jam.* Salem: Wellspring Studio, 2012, CD.
Stevenson, Brenda, ed. *The Journals of Charlotte Forten.* New York: Oxford
 Press, 1988.
Streeter, G.L. *Historical Collection of the Essex Institute Vol. II.* Published
 By Henry Whipple, Institute & Son, 1860.
Stevenson, Burton Egbert, Collected and edited by. *Other Sources: Poems of American
 History.* Boston: Houghton Mifflin Company, 1908 and reprinted 1922.

Tawa, Nicholas E. *Arthur Foote: A Musician of Frame in the Time and Place.*
 Lanham, Maryland: Scarecrow Press, Inc., 1997.

Valentine, Herbert E. *Dedication of the boulder commemorating the service of the
 Twenty-third Regiment, Massachusetts Volunteer Infantry, in the Civil War, 1861-
 1865, at Salem, Massachusetts, September 28, 1905. United States Army,
 Massachusetts Infantry Regiment, 23rd (1861 - 1865).* Salem, Mass.: Newcomb
 & Gauss, 1905.
Volo, D. D. *Family Life in Seventeenth and Eighteenth Century America.* Westport,
 CT: Greenwood Press, 2006.

Warner, Anne and Frank. *Traditional American Folk Songs.* Syracuse University
 Press, 1984.
Wells, S.R., ed. *Phrenological Journal and Packard's Monthly.* New York: Samuel R.
 Wells, Publisher, 389 Broadway, 1870.
Whittier, John Greenleaf. *The Complete Poetical Works of John Greenleaf Whittier.*
 Cambridge: Houghton Mifflin Company, 1894.
Willis, Lemuel. *A Semi-centennial Address Delivered in the Universalist Church, Salem,
 Mass., Thursday August 4, 1859, on the Occasion of Celebrating the 50th Anniversary
 of the dedication of the Church.* Salem: Charles W. Swasey, Register Press, 1859.

Zetzsche, and S. Knaebel. *Salem Independent Cadet Quick Step.* Boston: Stephen
 W. Marsh, monographic, 1848.

Web Resources

American Antiquarian Society
www.americanantiquarian.org

Ann Lewis Women's Suffrage Collection
www.lewissuffragecollection.omeka.net

Athlone Community Radio Podcast, The Bandmaster
www.athlonecommunityradio.ie

Broadside Ballads Bodleian Libraries Oxford University
www.ballads.bodleian.ox.ac.uk

Cecil Sharp House
www.vwml.org

Center for Popular Music, Middle Tennessee State University
www.popmusic.mtsu.edu

City of Salem
www.salem.com

Commonwealth Vintage Dancers
www. vintagedancers.org

Cyber Hymnal
www.hymntime.com

Dalton, Jim & Smith-Dalton, Maggi
www.singingstring.org

First Bullrun
www.firstbullrun.co.uk

Frederick E. Berry Library at Salem State University
www.salemstate.edu

Genealogy Wise
www.genealogywise.com

Google Books
www.books.google.com

Hadley Genealogy
www.hadleygenealogy.net

Hamilton Hall
www.hamiltonhall.org

Harris Broadside Collection, John Hay Library, Brown University
www.repository.library.brown.edu

Hathi Trust Digital Library
www.hathitrust.org

Historic Beverly
www.historicbeverly.net

History by the Sea
www.historybythesea.com

House of the Seven Gables
www.7gables.org

Hymnary
www.hymnary.org

Internet Archive
www.archive.org

Journal of American Folklore
www.jstor.org

Lester S. Levy Collection of Sheet Music, Johns Hopkins University
www.levysheetmusic.mse.jhu.edu

Library Company of Philadelphia
www.librarycompany.org

Library of Congress
www.loc.gov

Mainly Folk: English Folk and Other Good Music
www.mainlynorfolk.info

Mary Barker, Photographer
www.mabarkerphotography.com
Mass Moments
www.mass moments.org
Mudcat
www.mudcat.org
Music Score Library Project/ Petrucci Music Library
www.imslp.org
Music, Civil War
www.encyclopedia.com
Phillip's Library, Rowley/ Salem, Massachusetts
www.pem.org
Poetry & Song on the Outbreak of War
www.americainclass.org
Popular Songs of the Day
www.loc.gov
Protest Song Lyrics
www.protestsonglyrics.net
Registry of Deeds
www.salemdeeds.com
Rosie Strom - Graphic Designer
www.rosiestromdesign.com
Roud Folksong Index at the Vaughan Williams Memorial Library
www.vwml.org
Salem Links and Lore, Salem Public Library
www.noblenet.org
Salem Athenaeum
www.salemathenaeum.net
Salem, Massachusetts
www.salemweb.com
Streets of Salem
www.streetsofsalem.com

Traditional Ballad Index, Fresno State University
www.fresnostate.edu
Traditional Music Library
www.traditionalmusic.co.uk
Trial Pamphlets Collection, Cornell University Law Library
www.awcollections.library. cornell.edu
USGenNet
www.usgennet.org
Washington University Digital Gateway Image Collections & Exhibitions
www.lib-lslv126.wulib
Word on the Street
www.digital.nls.uk

Blogs

Escape Of Old John Webb
http://www.lazykacom/ linernotes/thesongs/ EscapeofOldJohn.htm
Rosanne Cash, Time Travel & the Ballad Tradition opinionator
https://opinionator.blogs. nytimes.com/2014/02/07/t ime-travel-and-the-ballad-tradition
Scottish Roots of Johnny Cash, the man in black tartan
www.theguardian.com/ music/2010/feb/07/johnny-cash scottish-roots

Chapter Tune References

Chapter 1: *Federal Street* by Henry K. Oliver. Music Score Library Project (IMSLP)/Petrucci Music Library, retrieved online July 20, 2017, www.imslp.org, Courtesy of the Petrucci Music Library.

Chapter 2: *Ring the Bell Softly, There's Crape on the Door* by Dexter Smith. Isiah Baltzell. *Excerpt from Gates of Praise: For the Sabbath-School, Praise-Service, Prayer-Meeting, Etc.* Dayton, OH: W. J. Shuey, 1884, 68.

Chapter 3: *Harmony Grove* by Henry K. Oliver. Lowell Mason. *Carmina Sacra: or Boston Collection of Church Music: comprising the most popular psalm and hymn Tunes in eternal use together with a great variety of new tunes, chants, sentences, motetts.* Boston: J. H. Wilkins & R. B. Carter, 1841, 63. Courtesy of the Boston Public Library.

Chapter 4: *Emancipation Hymn* by Manuel Fenollosa and R. T L., *Emancipation Hymn.* Boston: Oliver Ditson & Co., 1863, Notated Music, retrieved online July 20, 2017, http://www.loc.gov/item/ihas.200001094/.

Chapter 5: *Richmond March.* Jean M. Missud. Boston: F. Trifet Publisher. 1898, Duke University Digital Collection, retrieved online February 16, 2020, https://library.duke.edu/digitalcollections/hasm_b0906/

Chapter 6: *Salem Assemblies Waltzes.* Jean M. Missud. *Salem Assemblies Waltzes.* Oliver Ditson & Co., Boston, monographic, 1878. Notated Music, retrieved online February 16, 2020, https://www.loc.gov/item/sm1878.05436/.

Chapter 7: *Salem Willows For Mine.* Lou Collins, George Harry, Salem, Mass.: L.A. Collins, Publisher, 1919. Dee Dee Morneau's personal Collection.

Chapter 8: *Spring Song* by George Whitfield Chadwick. Dedicated to Salem Artist Ross Sterling Turner. Chadwick, G. W. *Spring Song.* Schmidt, Arthur P., Boston, monographic, 1882. Notated Music, retrieved online February 16, 2020, https://www.loc.gov/item/sm1882.20733/.

Chapter 9: *Walnut Grove* by Henry K. Oliver. Lowel Mason. *Carmina Sacra: or, Boston Collection of Church Music: comprising the most popular psalm and hymn tunes in eternal use together with a great variety of new tunes, chants, sentences, motetts.* Boston: J. H. Wilkins & R. B. Carter, 1841, 117. Courtesy of the Boston Public Library.

Chapter 10: *King Alcohol, a Temperance Glee.* (Boston: Oliver Diston, 135 Washington Street, 1843). Courtesy of Lester S. Levy Collection of Sheet Music, Sheridan Libraries, Johns Hopkins University.

NEW
FANEUIL
HALL
MARCH
FOR
PIANO
BY
JEAN M. MISSUD
WHITE-SMITH
MUSIC PUBLISHING CO.
BOSTON — NEW YORK — CHICAGO

HANDSOME
Sarah Jane!
COMPOSED BY HENRY O. UPTON,
And sung with unbounded applause by the Howard Burlesque Opera Troupe
of Salem, Mass. Words published by permission.

The moon was rising in the sky,
As Sarah came to me;
She asked if I would like to go
Down to the jubilee,
'Twas then I heard the banjo sound,
And also the tambourine;

Salem Witches
March
By JEAN M. MISSUD
Conductor of the Salem Cadet Band

Illustrated Title, 50c.   Band, 50c.
BOSTON

ROSALIE,
THE PRAIRIE FLOWER

On the distant prairie, where the heather
In its quiet beauty lived and smiled,
Stands a little cottage, and the creep
Loves around its porch to twine;
In that peaceful dwelling was a lovel
With her blue eyes beaming soft and
And the wavy ringlets of her flaxen
Floating in the summer air.

CHORUS.

Fair as a lily, joyous and free,
Light of that prairie home was she,
Every one who knew her felt the g
Of Rosalie, the Prairie Flower.

On that distant prairie, when the days we
Tripping like a fairy, sweet her song,
With the sunny blossoms, and the birds a
Beautiful and bright as they;
When the twilight shadows gathered in th
And the voice of nature sank to rest,
Like a cherub kneeling seemed the lovely
With her gentle eyes so mild.

Fair as a lily, &c.

But the summer ended, and the chilly blast,
O'er that peaceful cottage swept at last;
When the autumn song birds woke the dewy
Little Prairie Flower was gone.
For the angels whispered softly in her ear,
Child, thy Father calls thee, stay not here,
And they gently bore her, robed in spotless whi
To their peaceful home of light.

Fair as a lily, &c.

Published and sold wholesale and retail by
Joshua Peckham,
Dealer in CLOCKS, WATCHES, JEWELRY, FAN
CY GOODS, FIREWORKS, &c., &c.
187 Essex Street, Salem, Mass.

Photographs, Postcards, Clippings, Maps

Cover: *Pyncheon Lane Capric*, HOUSE OF THE SEVEN GABLES * *George A. Brown*, KENNETH S. GOLDSTEIN COLLECTION OF AMERICAN SONG BROADSIDES * Winter Island Lighthouse, MARY BARKER - Photographer * 1: *Federal Street*, Henry K. Oliver, Music Score, Library Project PETRUCCI MUSIC LIBRARY * 2: Salem Willows, SAL PANGALLO'S Personal Collection * 4: Pageant of Salem, SAL PANGALLO'S Personal Collection * 6: Henry K. Oliver, *Seventeenth Annual Report of the Bureau of Statistics of Labor*, SALEM PUBLIC LIBRARY HISTORICAL ROOM * 8: Cold Spring in North Salem, Salem Map 1874, BETSEY & ED BENNETT'S Personal Collection * 10: Chestnut Street, Salem, SAL PANGALLO'S Personal Collection * 11: Chestnut Street, Salem Map, 1874, BETSEY & ED BENNETT'S Personal Collection * 14: *Salem Hornpipe, Ryan's Mammoth Collection*, JIM and MAGGI DALTON'S Personal Collection * 15: *On the Road to Salem*, BOSTON PUBLIC LIBRARY * 16: SALEM ARTILLERY, T. WILLIAM SMITH * 17: *Be Salem Home, Essex Register*, CHRISTINE ELIZABETH MISTRETTA'S Personal Collection 18: *Ring The Bell Softly, There's Crape on the Door*, Dexter Smith, Isiah Baltzell. *Excerpt from Gates of Praise* BOSTON PUBLIC LIBRARY * 21: *Written on reading an account of the execution of Stephen M. Clark*, HARRIS BROADSIDE COLLECTION * 22: *George A. Brown*, KENNETH S. GOLDSTEIN COLLECTION OF AMERICAN SONG BROADSIDES * 23: Baker's Island, SAL PANGALLO'S Personal Collection * 25: *A Funeral Elegy*, LIBRARY OF CONGRESS * 29: *Murder of Joseph White*, HARRIS BROADSIDE COLLECTION * 30: Giles Corey Memorial, MARY BARKER - Photographer * 32: Dexter Smith, *PHRENOLOGICAL JOURNAL AND LIFE ILLUSTRATED* * 34: *Harmony Grove*, Henry K. Oliver, Lowell Mason's *Carmina*, BOSTON PUBLIC LIBRARY * 37: John Webb, *BOSTON EVENING POST*, BOSTON PUBLIC LIBRARY * 38: Original beams from the Salem Jail, NANCY LUTTS' Personal Collection * 40: 4 Federal Street, original sight of the Old Salem Jail, NANCY LUTTS' Private Collection * 42: The *Charlestown Land Shark*, HARRIS BROADSIDE COLLECTION * 44: Witch House, MARY BARKER - Photographer * 46: Witch House orginal location, SAL PANGALLO'S Personal Collection * 50: *Emancipation*

Hymn, LIBRARY OF CONGRESS * 52: Civil War Statue in Greenlawn Cemetery, MARY BARKER - Photographer * 54: *Get Off the Tracks*, LESTER S. LEVY COLLECTION OF SHEET MUSIC * 56: The Hutchinson Family Singers at Tabernacle Chapel in Salem, ANN LEWIS WOMEN'S SUFFRAGE COLLECTION * 59: Barton Square, Salem Map 1874, BETSEY & ED BENNETT'S Personal Collection * 62: Musical Entertainment at Mechanic Hall, Salem, CHRISTINE ELIZABETH MISTRETTA'S Private Collection* 63: *Cornerstone Hymn*, T. WILLIAM SMITH * 66: *Richmond March*, Jean M. Missud, DUKE UNIVERSITY DIGITAL COLLECTION * 68: *Departure of the Salem Light Infantry*, HARRIS BROADSIDE COLLECTION * 70: *Lines written for the Second Reunion of the 23rd Regiment*, KENNETH S. GOLDSTEIN COLLECTION OF AMERICAN SONG BROADSIDES * 71: Boulder Commemorating the Service of the 23rd Regiment, SAL PANGALLO'S Personal Collection * 73: *When Johnny Comes Marching Home*, JARLATH MACNAMARA'S Personal Collection * 74: *When Johnny Comes Marching Home*, JARLATH MACNAMARA'S Personal Collection *76: Grand Concert - Gilmore's Salem Brass Band, JARLATH MACNAMARA'S Personal Collection * 79: Joshua Ward House, 148 Washington Street, MARY BARKER - Photographer * 83: *Salem Mechanick Infantry Quick Step*, LESTER S. LEVY COLLECTION OF SHEET MUSIC * 83: *Salem Independent Cadet Quick Step*, LESTER S. LEVY COLLECTION OF SHEET MUSIC * 85: Leslie's Retreat, SAL PANGALLO'S Personal Collection * 88: *Song of the Minute Man*, HARRIS BROADSIDE COLLECTION * 92: *Salem Quick Step*, BOSTON PUBLIC LIBRARY * 92: Salem Cadet Band at Salem Willows, SAL PANGALLO'S Personal Collection * 93: *Salem Cadets' March*, BOSTON PUBLIC LIBRARY * 94: Pickering House, MARY BARKER - Photographer * 95: *Colonel Pickering's March to Lexington*, TRADITIONAL TUNE ARCHIVE * 96: *Dreaming of Home And Mother*, LIBRARY OF CONGRESS * 98: *God Bless America*, LIBRARY OF CONGRESS * 100: *Salem Assemblies Waltzes*, Jean Missud, LIBRARY OF CONGRESS * 102: Old Turnpike Guarded by Toll Gate, *SALEM EVENING NEWS* * 103: The Old Toll House, *SALEM EVENING NEWS* * 104: Old Salem Train Station, SAL PANGALLO'S Personal Collection * 106: *Hardware Advertisement, SALEM GAZETTE* * 107: Irish Turf, County Clare, Ireland, Author's Personal Collection

* 109: Barn Tools, Author's Personal Collection * 110: *The New England Blacking Man*, KENNETH S. GOLDSTEIN COLLECTION OF AMERICAN SONG BROADSIDES * 112: *Salem Willows For Mine*, Lou Collins and George Harry, DEE DEE MORNEAU'S Personal Collection * 116: Assembly House, SAL PANGALLO'S Personal Collection * 116: Assembly House, MARY BARKER - Photographer * 118: *Newhall's March*, FRED FINKLE * 119: *Lailson's Ride*, T. WILLIAM SMITH * 121: *Chestnut Street*, H.K. Oliver, BOSTON PUBLIC LIBRARY * 122: Hamilton Hall, SAL PANGALLO'S Private Collection * 122: Hamilton Hall, MARY BARKER - Photographer * 127: Music and Dancing Academy, *IMPARTIAL REGISTER* * 127: Walsh's Dancing Academy, *SALEM EVENING NEWS* * 127: Dancing and Dancing Academy, *SALEM GAZETTE* * 127: Dancing School, *SALEM GAZETTE* * 128: *Pyncheon Lane Capric*, HOUSE OF THE SEVEN GABLES * 130: *Salem Willows for Mine*, Lou Collins and George Harry, DEE DEE MORNEAU'S Personal Collection * 132: Salem Country Dance, AUTHOR'S Personal Collection * 133: *High Street*, T. WILLIAM SMITH * 134: *Spring Song*, George Whitfield Chadwick, LIBRARY OF CONGRESS * 140: *Twinkling Stars Are Laughing Love*, LESTER S. LEVY COLLECTION OF SHEET MUSIC * 142: *Belle of Tennessee A Plantation Song*, AUTHOR'S Personal Collection * 144: *Walnut Grove*, Henry K. Oliver, Lowell Mason's *Carmina*, BOSTON PUBLIC LIBRARY * 151: *Epitaph on a Favorite Pig*, *SALEM GAZETTE* * 152: *King Alcohol, a Temperance Glee*, LESTER S. LEVY COLLECTION OF SHEET MUSIC * 155: Father Mathew Statue, SAL PANGALLO'S Personal Collection * 161: Second Annual Picnic at Cabot Farm, NANCY LUTTS' Personal Collection * 163: *The Drunkard's Wish*, *SALEM GAZETTE* * 164: Father Mathew Statue, MARY BARKER - Photographer * 167: *The Last Glass*, HARRIS BROADSIDE COLLECTION * 168: Outlet Clothing House, JOANNA LISS' Personal Collection * 196: *Handsome Sarah Jane*, Henry Upton, LIBRARY COMPANY OF PHILADELPHIA, *Rosalie the Prairie Flower*, KENNETH S. GOLDSTEIN COLLECTION OF AMERICAN SONG BROADSIDE, *Salem Witches March*, Jean Missud, WASHINGTON UNIVERSITY DIGITAL GATEWAY IMAGE COLLECTIONS & EXHIBITIONS, *New Faneuil Hall March*, Jean Missud, LIBRARY OF CONGRESS * 200: 9th Annual Peace Pipes Concert, HAWC benefit, Author's Personal Collection

A benefit
concert 9th

Annual
Peace Pipes
Concert

An Evening of Scottish and Irish Music Featuring the
North Shore Pipe Band and Jen & Bob Strom

Saturday April 27 at 7:30 PM
Tabernacle Congregational Church, UCC
50 Washington Street, Salem MA

HAWC To benefit HAWC HAWC
(Healing Abuse Working for Change)
Salem-based domestic violence
prevention, education, and victim support

Suggested Donation $20
($10 Students and Seniors)

Index

- A -

- B -